A STRAIGHTFORWARD GUIDE TO YOUR RIGHTS AS A PRIVATE TENANT

ROGER SPROSTON

STRAIGHTFORWARD PUBLISHING
WWW.STRAIGHTFORWARDCO.CO.UK

Straightforward Publishing
Brighton BN2 4EG

© Straightforward Publishing 2005
Fifth Edition

All rights reserved. No part of this publication may be reproduced in a retrieval system or transmitted by any means, electronic or mechanical, photocopying or otherwise, without the prior permission of the copyright holder.

ISBN 1903909 59 7

Printed by Anthony Rowe Eastbourne

Cover design by Straightforward Graphics

The information in this book was correct at the time of going to print. The author and publishers cannot be held liable for any errors or omissions within or for any changes in law since publication.

CONTENTS

Introduction

1. Finding a property   9

Letting agents 9
Advertisements 10
Company lets 10
Short lets 11
Student lets 12
The DSS and Housing benefit 12
Holiday lets 13
Bedsits 14
Viewing a property 14

2. The law in a nutshell   15

Explaining the law 15
The freehold and the lease 15
Freehold 15
Leasehold 16
The position of the tenant 16
The tenancy agreement 17
The contract 17
Date of commencement and rent payable 17
Services provided under the tenancy 18
Tenants obligations 18
Landlords obligations 18
Ending a tenancy 18
Provision of a rent book 19
Overcrowding 20
Different types of tenancy agreement 20
The protected tenancy 20

	The assured tenancy	20
	Other types of agreement	21
	The squatter	21
3.	**Assured tenants**	**23**
	The assured tenant	23
	Tenancies that are not assured	24
	The assured shorthold tenancy	25
	Security of tenure	27
	The mandatory grounds for possession	27
	The discretionary grounds for possession	28
	Fast Track Possession	30
	Payment of rent	30
4.	**Joint tenancies**	**31**
5.	**Rent and other charges**	**33**
	Payment of rent	33
	The assured tenant	33
	Rent control for assured shorthold tenants	33
	Housing benefit	34
	Restrictions on the amount of benefit	35
	Council tax and the tenant	36
	Who has to pay council tax?	36
	Dwellings which are exempt	37
	Reductions in council tax	37
	Council tax and benefits	37
	Service charges	37
	Deposits	37
6.	**The right to quiet enjoyment of a home**	**41**
	Eviction and unlawful harassment	41

What can be done	43
The injunction	43
Damages	43

7. Repairs and improvements 45

Landlord and tenant obligations	45
Example of repairing responsibilities	45
Reporting repairs to a landlord	46
The tenants rights whilst repairs are carried out	47
Can the landlord increase the rent after doing repairs?	47
Tenants rights to make improvements	47
Disabled tenants	48
Shared housing	48
Sanitation health and hygiene	49
Renovation grants	49
Common parts grant	50

8. What should be provided under the tenancy 51

Furniture	51
Services	52
Repairs	52
Insurance	52
At the end of the tenancy	52

9. Going to court to regain possession of a home 55

10. Public sector tenancies 57

Secure tenancies	57
Right to buy	57
Rights to succeed to a secure tenancy	58
Right to repair and make improvements	58

Introductory tenancies	59
Housing association tenants	59

11. Private tenancies in Scotland 61

Protected tenancies	61
Grounds for possession	62
Fair rent system	62
Assured tenancies	62
Short assured tenancies	63

12. The Law and owner Occupiers 65

13. Obligations of freeholder and leaseholder 73

14. Owner occupiers and service charges 91

15. Enfranchisement and extension of leases 111

16. Relationship breakdown and housing rights 129

17. Housing Advice 135

Glossary of terms
Index

INTRODUCTION

This fifth edition of A Straightforward Guide to the Rights of the Private Tenant, substantially updates the previous edition by introducing more detailed information concerning the law, landlords obligations and tenants rights and obligations. It also introduces a new section on Leaseholders and commonholders.

Since the advent of the expansion in the buy-to-let sector, many people have become landlords and it is the case, unfortunately, that this expansion has introduced a lot of inexperienced people into the field. If an agent is used in the letting of property then there is usually no problem. However, when the property is directly managed then issues can arise that can lead to conflict.

The aim of this book is to ensure that all are clear about the law and practice of letting and residing in, private sector tenanted property.

The book covers the finding of a property, the law, detailed information on specific tenancies, payments of rent and benefits and repairing obligations. Issues such as unlawful eviction and harassment are covered, as are public sector tenancies plus tenancies in Scotland. There is a final section on the processes involved in regaining possession of a home for breach of tenancy.

The various notices used when going to court, and other forms associated with landlord and tenant can be obtained from the county courts. The internet site, www.court service.org can be accessed and all the necessary forms required in relation to housing matters can be downloaded for free. The court service website also gives a lot of valuable information in relation to housing.

The aim of this book is to inform the would-be tenant, or the landlord, about their rights and obligations and covers all areas in depth. It is to be hoped that an invaluable insight is gained and that both landlord and tenant can operate more effectively.

Roger Sproston
2005

1
FINDING A PROPERTY

Letting Agents
When looking for a property, there are obvious advantages in using an agent: they are likely to be experienced, can provide you with a tenancy agreement and they can provide a service after the property is let. It is important for a tenant to know that there will be a proper relationship between him/her and the landlord after moving in. Managing agents will provide this link.

Agents will typically look after the following:
- Transfer the utility bills and the council tax into the name of the tenant.
- Pay for repairs, although an agent will only normally do this if rent is being paid directly to them and they can make appropriate deductions.
- Chase rent arrears
- Serve notices of intent to seek possession if the landlord instructs them to do. An agent cannot commence court proceedings except through a solicitor.
- Visit the property at regular intervals check that the tenants are not causing any damage.
- Deal with neighbor complaints
- Bank rental receipts if the landlord is abroad
- Deal with housing benefit departments if necessary.

The extent to which agents actually do any or all of the following really depends on the caliber of the agent. It also depends on the type of agreement the landlord has with the agent.

Beware! There are many so-called rental agencies, which have sprung up since the property recession and also the advent of "Buy to Let". These agents are not professional, do not know a thing about property management, are shady and should be avoided like the plague. Shop around and seek a reputable agent.

Advertisements

The classified advertisement section of local papers is a good place to seek a property, local papers are obviously cheaper than the nationals such as the Evening Standard in London or the broadsheets such as the Guardian. The type of newspaper you look in will largely reflect what type of property you are looking for. An advert in the pages of the Times would indicate that the landlord is looking for a well-heeled professional and this would be reflected in the type of property that is to let.

Company lets

Where the tenant is a company rather than an individual, the tenancy agreement will be similar to an assured shorthold, but will not be bound by the six-month rule (see chapter 7 for details of assured shorthold tenancies). Company lets can be from any length of time, from a week to several years, or as long as you like.

The major difference between contracts and standard assured shorthold agreements is that the contract will be tailored to individual needs, and the agreement is bound by the provisions of contract law. Company tenancies are bound by the provisions of contract law and not by the 1988 Housing Act. Note: if you are a company and you are looking for a property to rent or let you must use a letting agent or solicitor.

The advantages of a landlord letting to a company are:

- A company or embassy has no security of tenure and therefore cannot be a sitting tenant.

- A company cannot seek to reduce the rent by statutory interventions.
- Rental payments are often made quarterly or six monthly in advance.
- The financial status of a company is usually more secure than that of an individual.
- Company tenants often require long term lets to accommodate staff relocating on contracts of between one and five years.

The main disadvantages of company lets are:

- A company tenancy can only be to a bona fide company or embassy, not to a private individual.
- A tenancy to a partnership would not count as a company let and may have some security of tenure.
- If the tenant is a foreign government, the diplomatic status of the occupant must be ascertained, as the courts cannot enforce breaches of contract with somebody who possesses diplomatic immunity.
- A tenancy to a foreign company not registered in the U.K may prove time consuming and costly if it becomes necessary to pursue claims for unpaid rent or damage through foreign courts.

Short lets

Although company lets can be of any length, it is becoming increasingly popular for companies to rent flats from private landlords on short lets.

A short let is any let of less than six months. But here, it is essential to check the rules with any borough concerned. Some boroughs will not allow lets for less than three months, as they do not want to encourage transient people in the neighborhood.

Generally speaking, short lets are only applicable in large cities where there is a substantial shifting population. Business executives on temporary relocation, actors and others involved in television production or film work, contract workers and visiting academics are examples of people who might require a short let. From a landlord's point of view, short lets are an excellent idea if you have to vacate your own home for seven or eight months, say, and do not want to leave it empty for that time. Short let tenants provide useful extra income as well as keeping an eye on the place. Or, if you are buying a new property and have not yet sold the old one, it can make good business sense to let it to a short let tenant.

Short let tenants are, usually, from a landlord's point of view, excellent blue-chip occupants. They are busy professionals, high earners, out all day and used to high standards. As the rent is paid by the company there is no worry for the landlord on this score either. A major plus of short lets is that they command between 20-50% more rent than the optimum market rent for that type of property. The one downside of short lets is that no agency can guarantee permanent occupancy.

Student lets
Many letting agencies will not consider students and a lot of landlords similarly are not keen. There is the perception that students will not look after a home and tend to live a lifestyle guaranteed to increase the wear and tear on a property. However, if handled correctly, student lets can be profitable. Although students quite often want property for only eight or nine months, agencies that deal with students make them sign for a whole year. Rent is guaranteed by confirmation that the student is a genuine student with references from parents, who act as guarantors. There can be a lot of money made from student lets. However, the tenancy will require more avid policing because of the nature of student lifestyle.

The DSS and housing benefit
Very few letting agencies or landlords will touch DSS or housing benefits tenants. However, as with student lets, there is another side of the coin.

Looking for a Property

Quite often it is essential for a tenant on HB to have a guarantor, usually a homeowner, before signing a tenancy. Then it is up to the machinations of the benefit system to ensure that the landlord receives rent. The rent is assessed by a benefit officer, with the rent estimated usually at market price. There are rent levels set for each are that the benefit officer will not go above.

A deposit is paid normally and rent is paid direct to the landlord. No other conditions can be accepted by a private landlord. Rent certainly cannot be paid direct to the tenant.

Although tenants on HB have a bad name, due to stereotyping, there are many reasons why a person may be on benefit and probably does not fit the picture of a scrounger who will trash a property. If housing benefit tenancies are manages well, then this can be a useful source of tenant.

Holiday lets

Before the Housing Act 1988 became law, many landlords advertised their properties as holiday lets to bypass the rules regarding security of tenure. Strictly speaking, a holiday let is a property let for no more than a month to any one tenant. If the same tenant renews for another month then the landlord is breaking the law. Nowadays, holiday lets must be just that-let for a genuine holiday.

Holiday lets are not covered by the Housing Act. The contract is finalized by exchange of letters with the tenant where they place a deposit and the owner confirms the booking. If the let is not for a genuine holiday you may have problems in evicting the tenant, as the whole point of a holiday let is that it is for no more than a fixed period of a month.

Generally speaking, certain services must be provided for the let to be deemed a holiday let. Cleaning services and changes of bed linen are essential. The amount paid by the holidaymaker will usually include utilities but would exclude use of the telephone, fax machine etc.

If possible, you should talk to someone with some experience of this type of let before entering into an agreement with an agency. The usual problems may arise, those of ensuring occupancy all year round and the maintenance of your property, which will be higher due to a high turnover.

Bedsits

Bedsitting rooms are usually difficult to let and can cause problems for tenants as well as landlords. It is best to leave this area of letting alone. There are numerous regulations to adhere to, Houses in Multiple Occupation regulations are quite strict. There is a problem also of high turnover. Leave this kind of letting to others and concentrate on houses or flats.

Viewing a property-The tenant

Once you have found a property, the next stage is to make arrangements for a viewing. It is a good idea to make all appointments on the same day in order to avoid wasting time. If you decide on a likely property, the landlord will wish to take up references, if an agency is not being used. This will normally be a previous landlord's reference and also a bank reference. Only when these have been received and it is established that the person(s) are safe will the letting go ahead. No keys will be handed over until the cheque has been cleared and the landlord is in receipt of a month's rent and a month's deposit.

In chapter two we will explore the legal framework governing residential lettings.

2

THE LAW IN A NUTSHELL

Explaining the law

As a tenant, or potential tenant, it is very important to understand the rights and obligations of both yourself and your landlord, exactly what can and what cannot be done once the tenancy agreement has been signed and you have moved into the property.

Some landlords think they can do exactly as they please, because the property belongs to them. Some tenants do not know any differently and therefore the landlord can, and often does, get away with breaking the law. However, this is not the case, there is a very strong legal framework governing the relationship between landlord and tenant and it is important that you have a grasp on the key principles of the law.

In order to fully understand the law we should begin by looking at the main types of relationship between people and their homes.

The freehold and the lease

In law, there are two main types of ownership and occupation of property. These are: freehold and leasehold. These arrangements are very old indeed. In the section dealing with the relationship between leaseholder and freeholder, towards the end of this book, we will be discussing leasehold and freehold in more depth.

Freehold

If a person owns their property outright (usually with a mortgage) then they are a freeholder. The only claims to ownership over and above their own might be those of the building society or the bank, which lent them the money to buy the place. They will re-possess the property if the mortgage payments are not kept up with.

In certain situations though, the local authority (council) for an area can affect a person's right to do what they please with their home even if they are a freeholder. This will occur when planning powers are exercised, for example, in order to prevent the carrying out of alterations without consent.

The local authority for your area has many powers and we will be referring to these regularly.

Leasehold

If a person lives in a property owned by someone else and has a written agreement allowing them to occupy the flat or house for a period of time i.e., giving them permission to live in that property, then they will, in the main, have a lease and either be a leaseholder or a tenant of a landlord.

The main principle of a lease is that a person has been given permission by someone else to live in his or her property for a period of time. The person giving permission could be either the freeholder or another leaseholder.

The tenancy agreement is one type of lease. If you have signed a tenancy agreement then you will have been given permission by a person to live in their property for a period of time.

The position of the tenant

The tenant will usually have an agreement for a shorter period of time than the typical leaseholder. Whereas the leaseholder will, for example, have an agreement for ninety-nine years, the tenant will have an agreement, which either runs from week to week or month to month (periodic tenancy) or is for a fixed term, for example, six-months or one-year.

These arrangements are the most common types of agreement between the private landlord and tenant.

The agreement itself will state whether it is a fixed term or periodic tenancy. If an agreement has not been issued it will be assumed to be a fixed term tenancy.

Both periodic and fixed term tenants will usually pay a sum of rent regularly to a landlord in return for permission to live in the property (more about rent and service charges later)

The tenancy agreement

The tenancy agreement is the usual arrangement under which one person will live in a property owned by another. Before a tenant moves into a property he/she will have to sign a tenancy agreement drawn up by a landlord or landlord's agent. *A tenancy agreement is a contract between landlord and tenant*

It is important to realize that when you sign a tenancy agreement, you have signed a contract with another person, which governs the way in which you will live in their property.

The contract

Typically, any tenancy agreement will show the name and address of the landlord and will state the names of the tenant(s). The type of tenancy agreement that is signed should be clearly indicated. This could be, for example, a Rent Act protected tenancy, an assured tenancy or an assured shorthold tenancy. In the main, in the private sector, the agreement will be an assured shorthold.

Date of commencement of tenancy and rent payable

The date the tenancy began and the duration (fixed term or periodic) plus the amount of rent payable should be clearly shown, along with who is responsible for any other charges, such as water rates, council tax etc, and a description of the property you are living in.

In addition to the rent that must be paid there should be a clear indication of when a rent increase can be expected. This information is sometimes shown in other conditions of tenancy, which should be given to the tenant when they move into their home. The conditions of tenancy will set out landlords and tenants rights and obligations.

Services provided under the tenancy and service of notice

If services are provided, i.e., if a service charge is payable, this should be indicated in the agreement. The tenancy agreement should indicate clearly the address to which notices on the landlord can be served by the tenant, for example, because of repair problems or notice of leaving the property. The landlord has a legal requirement to indicate this.

Tenants obligations

The tenancy agreement will either be a basic document with the above information or will be more comprehensive. Either way, there will be a section beginning "the tenant agrees." Here the tenant will agree to move into the property, pay rent, use the property as an only home, not cause a nuisance to others, take responsibility for certain internal repairs, not sublet the property, i.e., create another tenancy, and various other things depending on the property.

Landlords obligations

There should also be another section "the landlord agrees". Here, the landlord is contracting with the tenant to allow quiet enjoyment of the property. The landlord's repairing responsibilities are also usually outlined.

Ending a tenancy

Finally, there should be a section entitled "ending the tenancy" which will outline the ways in which landlord and tenant can end the agreement. It is in this section that the landlord should make reference to the "grounds for possession". Grounds for possession are circumstances where the landlord will apply to court for possession of his/her property. Some of these grounds relate to what is in the tenancy, i.e., the responsibility to pay rent and to not cause a nuisance.

Other grounds do not relate to the contents of the tenancy directly, but more to the law governing that particular tenancy. The grounds for possession are very important, as they are used in any court case brought against the tenant. Unfortunately, they are not always indicated in the tenancy agreement. As they are so important they are summarized later on in this chapter.

It must be said at this point that many residential tenancies are very light on landlord's responsibilities. Repairing responsibilities, and responsibilities relating to rental payment, are landlords obligations under law. This book deals with these, and other areas. However, many landlords will seek to use only the most basic document in order to conceal legal obligations.

The public sector tenancy (local authority or housing association), for example, is usually very clear and very comprehensive about the rights and obligations of landlord and tenant. Unfortunately, the private landlord often does not employ the same energy when it comes to educating and informing the tenant.

This is one of the main reasons for this book. It is essential that those who intend to let property for profit are able to manage professionally and set high standards as a private landlord. This is because the sector has been beset by rogues in the past. Correspondingly, as a tenant you need to know your rights very clearly and need to know how to enforce them.

The responsibility of the landlord to provide a tenant with a rent book

If the tenant is a weekly periodic tenant the landlord must provide him/her with a rent book and commits a criminal offence if he/she does not do so. This is outlined in the Landlord and Tenant Act 1985 sections 4 - 7. Under this Act any tenant can ask in writing the name and address of the landlord. The landlord must reply within twenty-one days of asking.

As most tenancies nowadays are fixed term assured shortholds then it is not strictly necessary to provide a tenant with a rent book. However, for the purposes of efficiency, and your own records, it is always useful to have a rent book and sign it each time rent is collected or a standing order is paid.

Overcrowding and the rules governing too many people living in the property

It is important to understand, when signing a tenancy agreement, that it is not permitted to allow the premises to become overcrowded, i.e., to allow more people than was originally intended, (which is outlined in the agreement) to live in the property. If a tenant does, then the landlord can take action to evict.

Different types of tenancy agreement

The protected tenancy - the meaning of the term

As a basic guide, if a person is a private tenant and signed their current agreement with a landlord before 15th January 1989 then they will, in most cases, be a protected tenant with all the rights relating to protection of tenure, which are considerable. Protection is provided under the 1977 Rent Act.

In practice, there are not many protected tenancies left and the tenant will usually be signing an assured shorthold tenancy. Nevertheless, we will be looking briefly at the Protected tenancy in the next chapter.

The assured shorthold tenancy - what it means

If the tenant entered into an agreement with a landlord after 15th January 1989 then they will, in most cases, be an assured tenant. We will discuss assured tenancies in more depth in chapter three. In brief, there are various types of assured tenancy. The assured shorthold is usually a fixed term version of the assured tenancy and enables the landlord to recover their property after six months and to vary the rent after this time.

At this point it is important to understand that the main difference between the two types of tenancy, protected and assured, is that the tenant has less rights as a tenant under the assured tenancy. For example, they will not be entitled, as is a protected tenant, to a fair rent set by a Rent Officer.

Other types of agreement

In addition to the above tenancy agreements, there are other types of agreement sometimes used in privately rented property. One of these is the company let, as we discussed in the last chapter, and another is the license agreement. The person signing such an agreement is called a licensee.

Licenses will only apply in special circumstances where the licensee cannot be given sole occupation of his home and therefore can only stay for a short period with minimum rights. It is not the intention to pursue licensees further in this book.

The squatter (trespasser)

In addition to the tenant and licensee, there is one other type of occupation of property, which needs mentioning. This is squatting. It is useful for the tenant to have a basic understanding of this area of occupation.

The squatter is usually someone who has gained entry to a vacant property, either a house or a flat, without permission.

Although the squatter, a trespasser, has the protection of the law and cannot be evicted without a court order, if he or she is to be given the protection of the law, the squatted property must have been empty in the first place.

On gaining entry to a property, the squatter will normally put up a notice claiming squatter's rights, which means that they are identifying themselves as a person or group having legal protection until a court order is obtained to evict them. Even if no notice is visible, the squatter has protection and it is an offence to attempt to remove them forcibly.

The squatter has protection from eviction under the Protection from Eviction Act 1977 and is also protected from violence or harassment by the Criminal Law Act of 1977. The trespasser who has entered an occupied property without permission has fewer rights. Usually, the police will either arrest or escort a trespasser off the premises. There is no protection from eviction. However, there is protection from violence and intimidation under the Criminal Law Act of 1977.

3

ASSURED TENANTS

The assured tenant
As we discussed in Chapter two, all tenancies, (with the exceptions detailed entered into after 15th January 1989), are known as assured tenancies. An assured shorthold, which is the most common form of tenancy used by the landlord nowadays, is one type of assured tenancy, and is for a fixed term of six months minimum and can be brought to an end with two months notice by serving a section 21 (of the Housing Act 1988) notice.

It is important to note that all tenancies signed after February 1997 are assured shorthold agreements unless otherwise stated.

Assured tenancies are governed by the 1988 Housing Act, as amended by the 1996 Housing Act. It is to these Acts, or outlines of the Acts that the tenant must refer when intending to sign a tenancy for a residential property.

For a tenancy to be assured, three conditions must be fulfilled:

1. The premises must be a dwelling house. This basically means any premises which can be lived in. Business premises will normally fall outside this interpretation.
2. There must exist a particular relationship between landlord and tenant. In other words there must exist a tenancy agreement. For example, a licence to occupy, as in the case of students, or accommodation occupied as a result of work, cannot be seen as a tenancy Following on from this, the accommodation must be let as a single unit. The tenant, who must be an individual, must normally be able to sleep, cook and eat in the accommodation. Sharing of

bathroom facilities will not prevent a tenancy being an assured tenancy but shared cooking or other facilities, such as a living room, will.
3. The third requirement for an assured tenancy is that the tenant must occupy the dwelling as his or her only or principal home. In situations involving joint tenants at least one of them must occupy.

Tenancies that are not assured

A tenancy agreement will not be assured if one of the following conditions applies:

-The tenancy or the contract was entered into before 15th January 1989;

-If no rent is payable or if only a low rent amounting to less than two thirds of the present ratable value of the property is payable;

-If the premises are let for business purposes or for mixed residential and business purposes;

-If part of the dwelling house is licensed for the sale of liquor for consumption on the premises. This does not include the publican who lets out a flat;

-If the dwelling house is let with more than two acres of agricultural land;

-If the dwelling house is part of an agricultural holding and is occupied in relation to carrying out work on the holding;
-If the premises are let by a specified institution to students, i.e., halls of residence;

-If the premises are let for the purpose of a holiday;

-Where there is a resident landlord, e.g., in the case where the landlord has let one of his rooms but continues to live in the house;

-If the landlord is the Crown (the monarchy) or a government department. Certain lettings by the Crown are capable of being assured, such as some lettings by the Crown Estate Commissioners;

-If the landlord is a local authority, a fully mutual housing association (this is where you have to be a shareholder to be a tenant) a newly created Housing Action Trust or any similar body listed in the 1988 Housing Act.

-If the letting is transitional such as a tenancy continuing in its original form until phased out, such as:

-A protected tenancy under the 1977 Rent Act;

-Secure tenancy granted before 1st January 1989, e.g., from a local authority or housing association. These tenancies are governed by the 1985 Housing Act).

The Assured Shorthold tenancy

The assured shorthold tenancy as we have seen, is the most common form of tenancy used in the private sector. The main principle of the assured shorthold tenancy is that it is issued for a period of six months minimum and can be brought to an end by the landlord serving two months notice on the tenant. At the end of the six-month period the tenant, if given two months prior notice, must leave.

Any property let on an assured tenancy can be let on an assured shorthold, providing the following three conditions are met:

- The tenancy must be for a fixed term of not less than six months.
- The agreement cannot contain powers which enable the

landlord to end the tenancy before six months. This does not include the right of the landlord to enforce the grounds for possession, which will be approximately the same as those for the assured tenancy (see below).
- A notice requiring possession at the end of the term is usually served two months before that date.
- A notice must be served before any rent increase giving one months clear notice and providing details of the rent increase.

If the landlord wishes to get possession of his/her property, in this case before the expiry of the contractual term, the landlord has to gain a court order. A notice of seeking possession must be served, giving fourteen days notice and following similar grounds of possession as an assured tenancy.

The landlord cannot simply tell a tenant to leave before the end of the agreed term.

If the tenancy runs on after the end of the fixed term then the landlord can regain possession by giving the required two months notice, as mentioned above.

At the end of the term for which the assured shorthold tenancy has been granted, the landlord has an automatic right to possession.

An assured shorthold tenancy will become periodic (will run from week to week) when the initial term of six months has elapsed and the landlord has not brought the tenancy to an end. A periodic tenancy is brought to an end with two months notice.

Assured shorthold tenants, can be evicted only on certain grounds some discretionary, some mandatory (see below).

In order for the landlord of an assured shorthold tenant to regain possession of the property, a notice of seeking possession (of property) must be served, giving fourteen days notice of expiry and stating the ground for possession. A copy of this notice is shown in Appendix 2. This notice is similar to a notice to quit, discussed in the previous chapter.

Following the fourteen days a court order must be obtained. Although gaining a court order is not complicated, a solicitor will

Assured Tenants

usually be used. Court costs can be awarded against the tenant. See appendix for particulars of claim.

Security of tenure: The ways in which a tenant can lose their home as an assured shorthold tenant

There are a number of circumstances called grounds (mandatory and discretionary) whereby a landlord can start a court action to evict a tenant.

The following are the *mandatory* grounds (where the judge must give the landlord possession) and *discretionary* grounds (where the judge does not have to give the landlord possession) on which a court can order possession if the home is subject to an assured tenancy.

The mandatory grounds for possession of a property let on an assured (shorthold) tenancy

There are eight mandatory grounds for possession, which, if proved, leave the court with no choice but to make an order for possession. It is very important that you understand these.

Ground One is used where the landlord has served a notice, no later than at the beginning of the tenancy, warning the tenant that this ground may be used against him/her.

This ground is used where the landlord wishes to recover the property as his or her principal (first and only) home or the spouse's (wife's or husbands) principal home. **The ground is not available to a person who bought the premises for gain (profit) whilst they were occupied.**

Ground Two is available where the property is subject to a mortgage and if the landlord does not pay the mortgage, could lose the home.
Grounds Three and Four relate to holiday lettings.
Ground Five is a special one, applicable to ministers of religion.
Ground Six relates to the demolition or reconstruction of the property.

Ground Seven applies if a tenant dies and in his will leaves the tenancy to someone else: but the landlord must start proceedings against the new tenant within a year of the death if he wants to evict the new tenant.

Ground Eight concerns rent arrears. This ground applies if, both at the date of the serving of the notice seeking possession and at the date of the hearing of the action, the rent is at least 8 weeks in arrears or two months in arrears. This is the main ground used by landlords when rent is not being paid.

The landlord should understand that in order to get a court order for possession of property for rent arrears then, because of the short-term nature of the Assured shorthold, time is of the essence. If the tenancy is into the third month, it may be easier to wait and serve a two-month notice of termination and get a court order against the occupants separately.

One of the advantages of a court order is that you will have details of the tenant's employers and can get an attachment of earnings against the tenant.

The discretionary grounds for possession of a property, which is let on an assured tenancy

As we have seen, the discretionary grounds for possession are those in relation to which the court has some powers over whether or not the landlord can evict. In other words, the final decision is left to the judge. Often the judge will prefer to grant a suspended order first, unless the circumstances are dramatic.

Ground Nine applies when suitable alternative accommodation is available or will be when the possession order takes effect. As we have seen, if the landlord wishes to obtain possession of his or her property in order to use it for other purposes then suitable alternative accommodation has to be provided.

Assured Tenants

Ground Ten deals with rent arrears as does *ground eleven*. These grounds are distinct from the mandatory grounds, as there does not have to be a fixed arrear in terms of time scale, e.g., 8 weeks. The judge, therefore, has some choice as to whether or not to evict. In practice, this ground will not be relevant to managers of assured shorthold tenancies.

Ground Twelve concerns any broken obligation of the tenancy. As we have seen with the protected tenancy, there are a number of conditions of the tenancy agreement, such as the requirement not to racially or sexually harass a neighbor. Ground Twelve will be used if these conditions are broken.

Ground Thirteen deals with the deterioration of the dwelling as a result of a tenant's neglect. This is connected with the structure of the property and is the same as for a protected tenancy. It puts the responsibility on the tenant to look after the premises.

Ground Fourteen concerns nuisance, annoyance and illegal or immoral use. This is where a tenant or anyone connected with the tenant has caused a nuisance to neighbors.

Ground 14A this ground deals with domestic violence.

Ground 15 concerns the condition of the furniture and tenants neglect. As Ground thirteen puts some responsibility on the tenant to look after the structure of the building so Ground Fifteen makes the tenant responsible for the furniture and fittings.

Ground 16 covers former employees. The premises were let to a former tenant by a landlord seeking possession and the tenant has ceased to be in that employment.

Ground 17 is where a person or that persons agents makes a false or reckless statement and this has caused the landlord to grant the tenancy under false pretences.

The description of the grounds above is intended as a guide only. For a fuller description please refer to the 1988 Housing Act, section 7, Schedule two,) as amended by the 1996 Housing Act) which is available at reference libraries.

Fast track possession

In November 1993, following changes to the County Court Rules, a facility was introduced which enabled landlords of tenants with assured shorthold tenancies to apply for possession of their property without the usual time delay involved in waiting for a court date and attendance at court. This is known as "fast track possession" It cannot be used for rent arrears or other grounds. It is used to gain possession of a property when the fixed term of six months or more has come to an end and the tenant will not move.

Payment of rent

If the landlord wishes to raise rent, at least one month's minimum notice must be given. The rent cannot be raised more than once for the same tenant in one year. Tenants have the right to challenge a rent increase if they think it is unfair by referring the rent to a Rent Assessment Committee. The committee will prevent the landlord from raising the rent above the ordinary market rent for that type of property. We will be discussing rent and rent control further on in this book.

4

JOINT TENANCIES

Joint tenancies tenancies: the position of two or more people who have a tenancy agreement for one property

Although it is the normal state of affairs for a tenancy agreement, to be granted to one person, this is not always the case.

A tenancy can also be granted to two or more people and is then known as a *joint tenancy*. The position of joint tenants is exactly the same as that of single tenants. In other words, there is still one tenancy even though it is shared.

Each tenant is responsible for paying the rent and observing the terms and conditions of the tenancy agreement. No one joint tenant can prevent another joint tenants access to the premises.

If one of the joint tenants dies then his or her interest will automatically pass to the remaining joint tenants. A joint tenant cannot dispose of his or her interest in a will.

If one joint tenant, however, serves a notice to quit (notice to leave the property) on another joint tenant(s) then the tenancy will come to an end and the landlord can apply to court for a possession order, if the remaining tenant does not leave.

The position of a wife or husband in relation to joint tenancies is rather more complex because the married person has more rights when it comes to the home than the single person.

Remember: the position of a tenant who has signed a joint tenancy agreement is exactly the same as that of the single tenant. If one person leaves, the other(s) have the responsibilities of the tenancy. If one person leaves without paying his share of the rent then the other tenants will have to pay instead.

5
RENT AND OTHER CHARGES

The payment of rent and other financial matters
If a tenancy is protected under the Rent Act 1977, as described earlier there is the right to apply to the Rent Officer for the setting of a fair rent for the property.

The assured tenant
The assured tenant has far fewer rights in relation to rent control than the protected tenant.

The Housing Act 1988 allows a landlord to charge whatever he likes. There is no right to a fair or reasonable rent with an assured tenancy. If the tenancy is assured then there will usually be a formula in the tenancy which will provide guidance for rent increases. If not then the landlord can set what rent he or she likes within reason. If the amount is unreasonable then the tenant can refer the matter to the rent assessment committee. The rent can sometimes be negotiated at the outset of the tenancy. This rent has to be paid as long as the contractual term of the tenancy lasts. Once the contractual term has expired, the landlord is entitled to continue to charge the same rent.

On expiry of an assured shorthold the landlord is free to grant a new tenancy and set the rent to a level that is compatible with the market.

Rent control for assured shorthold tenants
We have seen that the assured shorthold tenancy is for a period of six months minimum. Like the assured tenant, the assured shorthold tenant has no right to request that a fair rent should be set. The rent is a market rent.

As with an assured tenancy, the assured shorthold tenant has the right to appeal to a Rent Assessment Committee in the case of what he/she considers an unreasonable rent. This may be done during the contractual term of the tenancy. The Committee will consider whether the rent is significantly higher than is usual for a similar property.

If the Committee assess a different rent from that set by the landlord, they may set a date when the increase will take effect. The rent cannot be backdated to before the date of the application. Once a decision has been reached by the Committee, the landlord cannot increase the rent for at least twelve months, or on termination of the tenancy.

Details of the local Rent Assessment Committee can be obtained from the Rent Officer Service at your local authority.

Housing benefit

Housing benefit is a means tested benefit available only to tenants who cannot pay their rent. It is available whether or not the tenant is in employment. Housing benefit is administered by the local authority who are in turn reimbursed by central government.

Local authorities will assess the level of rent in their areas. They use what are known as reference rents and will not pay above this level. This was introduced to curb excessive rents. In addition, rent will normally be paid to landlords direct in order to ensure that rent is paid and not spent on other things.

The rules for entitlement to housing benefit differ according to whether the tenant is in receipt of income support. In the case of income support, entitlement to housing benefit is automatic and the maximum benefit will be payable. For other claimants, entitlement is means tested and the general principle is that over a certain personal earnings limit corresponding reductions will apply. It is not only the claimants income that is relevant: capital over a certain limit will be deemed to be income. Also, other people living in the home will affect entitlement.

The basic rule for housing benefit is that the property must be the only or principal home, although temporary absence can be ignored. Entitlement to benefit is based on the amount of 'eligible' rent. This

Rent and Other Charges

means that certain personal items, such as heating, lighting and water charges will not be eligible for rent.

Restrictions on the amount of benefit

As mentioned, the benefit payable may not be the full amount of eligible rent. This is to discourage claims for excessively large properties and high rents. The principle is that benefit is paid according to need. The rules governing the amount paid differ depending upon whether the applicant first became entitled to benefit before 2nd January 1996 or afterwards.

Previously, private sector rents were referred to the rent officer to determine whether or not they were a reasonable market rent. This no longer happens. In determining the reasonable market rent the rent officer will also take into account the size factor, the criteria of which are laid down. If the accommodation is significantly larger than the tenant and family, if relevant, need then the rent officer can set a lower figure, based on need. Local authorities will not always automatically limit the rent paid as they will, as appropriate take into account the needs of the family, for example disability.

The size criteria for calculating benefit are:

a) One bedroom for each of the following category of occupiers:
- A married or unmarried couple
- A person who is not a child
- Two children of the same sex
- Two children who are less than 10 years old
- A child (person under 16)

b) The number of rooms (excluding any allowed as a bedroom) suitable for living in:

- For fewer than four occupants, one
- For more than three but fewer than seven occupants, two

• In any other case, three.

Local authorities are asked to set a 'local reference rent' for the area. This is the average rent which the rent officer would expect a landlord to be able to obtain on a letting of a property in that locality to a tenant not claiming benefit. Rents are set on a needs basis. There are other formula applied to the payment of housing benefit and the local authority will inform you of the criteria used on application for benefit.

Council tax and the tenant
From April 1993 the council tax replaced the poll tax. Unlike poll tax, the council tax is based on properties, or dwellings, and not individual people. This means that there is one bill for each individual dwelling, rather than separate bills for each person. The number and type of people who live in the dwelling may affect the size of the final bill. A discount of 25% is given for people who live alone. Each property is placed in a valuation band with different properties paying more or less depending on their individual value. Tenants who feel that their home has been placed in the wrong valuation band can appeal to their local authority council tax department.

Who has to pay the council tax?
In most cases the tenant occupying the dwelling will have to pay the council tax. However, a landlord will be responsible for paying the council tax where there are several households living in one dwelling. This will usually be hostels, bedsits and other non-self contained flats where people share things such as cooking and washing facilities. The council tax on this type of property remains the responsibility of the landlord even if all but one of the tenants move out. Although the landlord has the responsibility for paying the council tax, he/she will normally try to pass on the increased cost through rents. However, as we have seen, there is a set procedure for a landlord to follow if he/she wishes to increase rent.

Rent and Other Charges

Dwellings, which are exempt

Certain properties will be exempt from the council tax, such as student's halls of residences and nurse's homes. Properties with all students resident will be exempt from the tax. However, if one non-student moves in then that property will no longer be exempt from tax. Uninhabitable empty properties are exempt from tax, as they are not counted as dwellings. This is not the same as homes, which have been declared as unfit for human habitation by Environmental Health officers. The deciding factor will be whether or not a property is capable of being lived in.

Reductions in council tax bills

Tenants in self-contained accommodation who live alone will be entitled to a discount of 25% of the total bill. Tenants may also qualify for the discount if they share their homes with people who do not count for council tax purposes. Such people are: children under eighteen; students; patients resident in hospital; people who are severely mentally impaired; low paid careworkers; eighteen or nineteen year olds still at school (or just left); people in prison (except for non-payment of fines or the council tax); and people caring for someone with a disability who is not a spouse, partner or child under eighteen.

Council tax benefits available for those on low income

Tenants on very low income, except for students, will usually be able to claim council tax benefit. This can cover up to 100% of the council tax. Tenants with disabilities may be entitled to further discounts. Tenants who are not responsible for individual council tax, but pay it through their rent, can claim housing benefit to cover the increase.

The rules covering council tax liability can be obtained from a Citizens Advice Bureau or from your local authority council tax department.

Service charges

A service charge covers provision of services other than those covered by the rent. A rental payment will normally cover maintenance charges, loan charges if any, and also profit. Other services, such as cleaning and gardening, will be covered by a separate charge, known as a service charge. A *registered* rent reflects the cost of any services provided by the landlord. An assured rent set by a landlord will normally include services, which must be outlined in the agreement.

The fact that the charges are variable must be written into a tenancy agreement and the landlord has a legal duty to provide the tenant with annual budgets and accounts and has to consult when he or she wishes to spend over a certain amount of money, currently £250 per dwelling.

The form of consultation, which must take place, is that of writing to all those affected and informing them of:

The landlord's intention to carry out work;

Why these works are seen to be necessary;

The estimated cost of the works;

At least two estimates or the inviting of them to see two estimates.

A period of twenty-eight days must be allowed for consideration and a further twenty eight before work is carried out. This gives time for any feedback from tenants.

The landlord can incur reasonable expense, without consultation, if the work is deemed to be necessary, i.e. emergency works.

If a service charge is variable then a landlord has certain legal obligations, which are clearly laid out in the 1985 and 1987 Landlord and Tenant Acts, as amended by the 2003 Leasehold and Commonhold Reform Act.

Deposits

A landlord can charge a *deposit*, to set against the possibility that a tenant may damage the property or furniture. For most types of tenancy the law puts a limit on the amount that can be charged. The normal amount is 1 month's rent.

6

THE RIGHT TO QUIET ENJOYMENT OF A HOME

Earlier, we saw that when a tenancy agreement is signed, the landlord is contracting to give quiet enjoyment of the tenants home. This means that they have the right to live peacefully in the home without harassment.

The landlord is obliged not to do anything that will disturb the right to the quiet enjoyment of the home. The most serious breach of this right would be for the landlord to wrongfully evict a tenant.

Eviction: what can be done against unlawful harassment and eviction

It is a criminal offence for a landlord unlawfully to evict a residential occupier (whether or not a tenant!). The occupier has protection under the Protection from Eviction Act 1977 section 1(2).

If the tenant or occupier is unlawfully evicted his/her first course should be to seek an injunction compelling the landlord to readmit him/her to the premises. It is an unfortunate fact but many landlords will attempt to evict tenants forcefully. In doing so they break the law.

However, the landlord may, on termination of the tenancy recover possession without a court order if the agreement was entered into after 15th January 1989 and it falls into one of the following six situations:

- The occupier shares any accommodation with the landlord and the landlord occupies the premises as his or her only or principal home.
- The occupier shares any of the accommodation with a member

of the landlords family, that person occupies the premises as their only or principal home, and the landlord occupies as his or her only or principal home premises in the same building.

- The tenancy or licence was granted temporarily to an occupier who entered the premises as a trespasser.

- The tenancy or licence gives the right to occupy for the purposes of a holiday.

- The tenancy or licence is rent-free.

- The licence relates to occupation of a hostel.

There is also a section in the 1977 Protection from Eviction Act which provides a defense for otherwise unlawful eviction and that is that the landlord may repossess if it is thought that the tenant no longer lives on the premises. It is important to note that, in order for such action to be seen as a crime under the 1977 Protection from Eviction Act, the intention of the landlord to evict must be proved.

However, there is another offence, namely harassment, which also needs to be proved. Even if the landlord is not guilty of permanently depriving a tenant of their home he/she could be guilty of harassment.

Such actions as cutting off services, deliberately allowing the premises to fall into a state of disrepair, or even forcing unwanted sexual attentions, all constitute harassment and a breach of the right to *quiet enjoyment*.

The 1977 Protection from Eviction Act also prohibits the use of violence to gain entry to premises. Even in situations where the landlord has the right to gain entry without a court order it is an offence to use violence.

If entry to the premises is opposed then the landlord should gain a court order.

What can be done against unlawful evictions?

There are two main remedies for unlawful eviction: damages and, as stated above, an injunction.

The injunction

An injunction is an order from the court requiring a person to do, or not to do something. In the case of eviction the court can grant an injunction requiring the landlord to allow a tenant back into occupation of the premises. In the case of harassment an order can be made preventing the landlord from harassing the tenant.

Failure to comply with an injunction is contempt of court and can result in a fine or imprisonment.

Damages

In some cases the tenant can press for *financial compensation* following unlawful eviction. Financial compensation may have to be paid in cases where financial loss has occurred or in cases where personal hardship alone has occurred.

The tenant can also press for *special damages*, which means that the tenant may recover the definable out-of-pocket expenses. These could be expenses arising as a result of having to stay in a hotel because of the eviction. Receipts must be kept in that case. There are also *general damages*, which can be awarded in compensation for stress, suffering and inconvenience.

A tenant may also seek *exemplary damages* where it can be proved that the landlord has disregarded the law deliberately with the intention of making a profit out of the displacement of the tenant.

7
REPAIRS AND IMPROVEMENTS

Repairs and improvements generally: the landlord and tenants obligations

Repairs are essential works to keep the property in good order. Improvements are alterations to the property, e.g. the installation of a shower.

As we have seen, some tenancies are periodic, week-to-week or month-to-month. If a tenancy falls into this category, or is a fixed-term tenancy for less than seven years, and began after October1961, then a landlord is legally responsible for most major repairs to the flat or house. Repairs are paid for out of your rent.

If a tenancy began after 15th January 1989 then, in addition to the above responsibility, the landlord is also responsible for repairs to common parts and service fittings.

The area of law dealing with the landlord and tenants repairing obligations is the 1985 Landlord and Tenant Act, section 11.

This section of the Act is known as a covenant and cannot be excluded by informal agreement between landlord and tenant. In other words the landlord is legally responsible whether he or she likes it or not. Parties to a tenancy, however, may make an application to a court mutually to vary or exclude this section.

An example of repairs a landlord is responsible for:
Leaking roofs and guttering;
Rotting windows;
Rising damp;
Damp walls;

Faulty electrical wiring;
Dangerous ceilings and staircases;
Faulty gas and water pipes;
Broken water heaters and boilers;
Broken lavatories, sinks or baths.

In shared housing the landlord must see that shared halls, stairways, kitchens and bathrooms are maintained and kept clean and lit.

Normally, tenants are responsible only for minor repairs, e.g., broken door handles, cupboard doors, etc. Tenants will also be responsible for decorations unless they have been damaged as a result of the landlord's failure to do repair.

A landlord will be responsible for repairs only if the repair has been reported. It is therefore important to report repairs in writing and keep a copy. If the repair is not carried out then action can be taken. Damages can also be claimed.

Compensation can be claimed, with the appropriate amount being the reduction in the value of the premises to the tenant caused by the landlord's failure to repair. If the tenant carries out the repairs then the amount expended will represent the decrease in value.

The tenant does not have the right to withhold rent because of a breach of repairing covenant by the landlord. However, depending on the repair, the landlord will not have a very strong case in court if rent is withheld.

REPORTING REPAIRS TO A LANDLORD

The tenant has to tell the landlord or the person collecting the rent straight away when a repair needs doing. It is advisable that it is in writing, listing the repairs that need to be done.

Once a tenant has reported a repair the landlord must do it within a reasonable period of time. What is reasonable will depend on the nature of the repair. If certain emergency work needs to be done by the council, such as leaking guttering or drains a notice can be served ordering the landlord to do the work within a short time. In exceptional cases if a home cannot be made habitable at reasonable cost the council may declare that the house must no longer be used, in which case the council has a legal duty to re-house a tenant.

If after the council has served notice the landlord still does not do the work, the council can send in its own builder or, in some cases take the landlord to court. A tenant must allow a landlord access to do repairs. The landlord has to give twenty-four hours notice of wishing to gain access.

The tenants rights whilst repairs are being carried out

The landlord must ensure that the repairs are done in an orderly and efficient way with minimum inconvenience to the tenant If the works are disruptive or if property or decorations are damaged the tenant can apply to the court for compensation or, if necessary, for an order to make the landlord behave reasonably.

If the landlord genuinely needs the house empty to do the work he/she can ask the tenant to vacate it and can if necessary get a court order against the tenant.

A *written agreement* should be drawn up making it clear that the tenant can move back in when the repairs are completed and stating what the arrangements for fuel charges and rent are.

If a person is an *assured* tenant the landlord could get a court order to make that person give up the home permanently if there is work to be done with him/her in occupation in occupation.

Can the landlord put the rent up after doing repairs?

If there is a service charge for maintenance, the landlord may be able to pass on the cost of the work(s).

Tenants rights to make improvements to a property

Unlike carrying out repairs the tenant will not normally have the right to insist that the landlord make actual alterations to the home. However, a tenant needs the following amenities and the law states that you should have them:

Bath or shower;
Wash hand basin;
Hot and cold water at each bath, basin or shower;
An indoor toilet.

If these amenities do not exist then the tenant can contact the council's Environmental Health Officer. An improvement notice can be served on the landlord ordering him to put the amenity in.

Disabled tenants

If a tenant is disabled he/she may need special items of equipment in the accommodation. The local authority may help in providing and, occasionally, paying for these. The tenant will need to obtain the permission of the landlord. If you require more information then contact the social services department locally.

Shared housing. The position of tenants in shared houses (Houses in Multiple Occupation)

The law lays down special standards for shared housing (houses in multiple occupation). These are usually bedsit houses of more than four people. Local authorities have special powers to deal with bad conditions when they occur. The legal regulations for houses in multiple occupation are set out in the Housing (Management of Houses in Multiple Occupation) Regulations 1990 and also the Housing Act 1996. Recent legislation has also been enacted.

The manager of a house in multiple occupation has responsibilities under the management regulations to carry out repair, maintenance and cleaning work and also safety work necessary to protect residents from risk of injury. A notice must be displayed where all the residents can see it showing the name, address and telephone number of the manager. Landlords must ensure that main entrances shared passageways, staircases and other common areas are maintained. All services such as gas, electricity and water supplies, plus drainage facilities, must also be maintained.

The same rules apply to the internal areas of living accommodation. In addition, there is a duty to maintain adequate fire safety, as obviously, shared housing is at greater risk of fire. Self-closing fire doors, emergency escape lighting, fire alarms and detectors and fire fighting equipment will normally be required. Signs indicating fire escape routes must be displayed where they are easy to see.

There are also rules concerning overcrowding in shared housing. The local authority has powers to tackle overcrowding problems; landlords, on request, have to supply the local authority with numbers of individuals and households in a shared house. Tenants also have duties, which enable landlords to fulfill their legal responsibilities. Tenants should allow landlords access at reasonable times, give details of all who live in the accommodation, and take care to avoid damage to property.

Sanitation health and hygiene

Local authorities have a duty to serve an owner with a notice requiring the provision of WCs when a property has insufficient sanitation, sanitation meaning toilet waste disposal.

They will also serve notice if it is thought that the existing sanitation is inadequate and is harmful to health or is a nuisance.

Local authorities have similar powers under various Public Health Acts to require owners to put right bad drains and sewers, also food storage facilities and vermin, plus the containing of disease.

The Environmental Health Department, if it considers the problem bad enough will serve a notice requiring the landlord to put the defect right. In certain cases the local authority can actually do the work and require the landlord to pay for it. This is called work *in default*.

Renovation grants

In certain cases the local authority will give assistance towards essential works on properties. Usually it is a part *grant* and is *means tested*; i.e. the amount you get depends on income.

There are different kinds of help to suit different needs, depending on the type of property involved and the scale of the work you may want to carry out.

Grants may be available towards the cost of repairs, improvements, and conversions of buildings and of providing facilities and adaptations for disabled people. In addition, minor assistance may also be available to help some tenants who want to carry out small-scale work on their homes.

There are certain circumstances where a tenant, can apply for a grant. In a lot of cases a landlord would apply because it is his/her property. The types of work which attract grant are as follows:

Renovation grant

The main purpose for which renovation grant is intended is to bring a property up to the standard of fitness for human habitation: this includes bringing properties back up to a certain standard. Therefore typical work would be home insulation and for heating, for providing satisfactory internal arrangements and for conversions (of old houses).

The amount of grant available will be determined by the central and local government policy then in force and will almost certainly be means-tested.

Common parts grant

There is another form of grant available, the common parts grant which is applicable to blocks of flats, or houses converted into flats. Both landlord and tenant together can apply for this type of grant. Occupying tenants can apply for this grant together, without the landlord, provided that they are all liable under the terms of the tenancy agreement. Again, this grant is means-tested and is a partial grant.

There are other forms of grant available but in the main only a landlord would apply for them, such as a houses in multiple occupation grant. In this book, there is space only or the briefest of outlines concerning the availability of grants. The first point of enquiry in relation to grants should be your local authority, which can advise you further.

8
WHAT SHOULD BE PROVIDED UNDER THE TENANCY

Furniture

A landlords decision whether or not to furnish property will depend on the sort of tenant that he is aiming to find. The actual legal distinction between a furnished property and an unfurnished property has faded into insignificance.

If a landlord does let a property as furnished then the following would be the absolute minimum:

- Seating, such as sofa and armchair

- Cabinet or sideboard

- Kitchen tables and chairs

- Cooker and refrigerator

- Bedroom furniture

Even unfurnished lets, however, are expected to come complete with a basic standard of furniture, particularly carpets and kitchen goods. If the landlord does supply electrical equipment then he or she is able to disclaim any repairing responsibility for it, but this must be mentioned in the tenancy agreement.

Services

Usually, a landlord will only provide services to a tenant if the property is a flat situated in a block or is a house on a private estate. The services will include cyclical painting and maintenance, usually on a three to four year basis (flats) and gardening and cleaning plus repairs to the communal areas, plus communal electricity bills and water rates. These services should be outlined in the agreement and are administered within a strict framework of law, The 1985 Landlord and Tenant Act Section 18-30 as amended by the 1987 LTA, the 1996 Housing Act and the 20032 Commonhold and Leasehold Reform Act.. The landlord has rigid duties imposed within these Acts, such as the need to gain estimates before commencing works and also to consult with residents where the cost exceeds £250 per flat. The landlord must give the tenant 28 days notice of works inviting feedback and then a further 28 days before works commence. Tenants have the right to see audited accounts and invoices relating to work. Service charges, as an extra payment over and above the rent are always contentious and it is an area that Landlords need to be aware of if they are to manage professionally.

Repairs

See chapter on repairing obligations

Insurance

Strictly speaking, there is no duty on either landlord or tenant to insure the property. However, it is highly advisable for the landlord to provide buildings insurance as he/she stands to lose a lot more in the event of fire or other disaster than the tenant. A landlord letting property for a first time would be well advised to consult his/ her insurance company before letting as there are different criteria to observe when a property is let and not to inform the company could invalidate the policy.

At the end of the tenancy

The tenancy agreement will normally spell out the obligations of the tenant at the end of the term. Essentially, the tenant will have an obligation to:

What Should be Provided under the Tenancy

- have kept the interior clean and tidy and in a good state of repair and decoration
- have not caused any damage
- have replaced anything that they have broken
- replace or pay for the repair of anything that they have damaged
- pay for the laundering of the linen
- pay for any other laundering
- put anything that they have moved or removed back to how it was

Sometimes a tenancy agreement will include for the tenants paying for anything that is soiled at their own expense, although sensible wear and tear is allowed for.

The landlord will normally be able to recover any loss from the deposit that the tenant has given on entering the premises. However, sometimes, the tenants will withhold rent for the last month in order to recoup their deposit. It is up to the landlord to negotiate re-imbursement for any damage caused, but this should be within reason. There is a remedy, which can be pursued in the Small Claims court if the tenants refuse to pay but this is rarely successful.

9

GOING TO COURT TO REGAIN POSSESSION OF A HOME

There may come a time when the landlord needs to go to court to regain possession of his property. This will usually arise when the contract has been breached by the tenant, for non-payment of rent or for some other breach such as nuisance or harassment. As we have seen, a tenancy can be brought to an end in a court on one of the grounds for possession. However, as the tenancy will usually be an assured shorthold then it is necessary to consider whether you are in a position to be given two months notice, as opposed to going to court.

If the landlord decides, for whatever reasons, to go to court, then any move to regain a property for breach of agreement will commence in the county court in the area in which the property is. The first steps in ending the tenancy will necessitate the serving of a notice of seeking possession using one of the Grounds for Possession detailed earlier in the book. If the tenancy is protected then 28 days must be given, the notice must be in prescribed form and served on the tenant personally. See appendix for sample notice seeking possession.

If the tenancy is assured shorthold, which is more often the case now, then 14 days notice of seeking possession can be used. In all cases the ground to be relied upon must be clearly outlined in the notice.

If the case is more complex, then this will entail a particulars of claim being prepared, usually by a solicitor, as opposed to a standard possession form.

A fee is paid when sending the particulars to court, which is currently £150. The standard form which the landlord uses for routine rent arrears cases is called the N5 (see appendix) and there will be an accompanying Particulars of Claim. Both of these forms can be obtained from the court. When completed, the forms should be sent in duplicate to the county court and a copy retained for you.

The court will send a copy of the Particulars of claim and the summons to the tenant. They will send a form which gives the landlord a case number and court date to appear, known as the return date.

On the return date, if you are defending yourself (see form of defence in appendix) you should arrive at court at least 15 minutes early. You can represent yourself in simple cases but are advised to use a solicitor for more contentious cases.

A number of orders are available. However, if the landlord has gone to court on the mandatory ground eight then if the fact is proved then he will get possession immediately. If not, then the judge can grant an order, suspended whilst the tenant finds time to pay.

Whatever the order, a bailiff warrant will be needed to finally evict the tenant from the property. This can be obtained after the order is given by filling in the appropriate form and paying a fee to the bailiff office.

In a lot of cases, it is more expedient for a landlord to serve notice-requiring possession, if the tenancy has reached the end of the period, and then wait two months before the property is regained. This saves the cost and time of going to court particularly if the ground is one of nuisance or other, which will involve solicitors.

If a tenancy has reached the end of the contractual term and the landlord wish's to recover his property then a "fast track" procedure is available which entails gaining an order for possession and bailiff's order by post. This can be used in cases with the exception of rent arrears.

10
PUBLIC SECTOR TENANCIES

Lettings of property by public sector landlords such as local authorities are specifically excluded from being assured tenancies under the 1988 Housing Act or protected tenancies under the 1977 Rent Act. Some Housing Associations with older tenancies also have this restriction.

Tenancies signed by Local authority tenants are known as secure tenancies and are protected by the 1985 Housing Act.

Secure Tenancies
Secure tenants have security of tenure under the 1985 Housing Act. This means that they cannot be evicted without a court order. However, security can be lost if the following circumstances arise:
- A tenant ceases to use the home as his/her only or principal home. This means that the property let under a secure tenancy should be lived in 80% of the time
- If a property is sub-let without permission then security is lost
- If a property is abandoned then security is lost unless the tenant can demonstrate a clear intention to return.

A secure tenant has many rights over and above those of an assured tenant. There is the right to buy a property, the right to mutually exchange with someone else, the right to sub-let with permission and the right to succeed to a tenancy on death or by assignment.

Right-to-buy.
Perhaps the most valuable right enjoyed by a secure tenant is the right to buy either the freehold, in the case of a house, or the leasehold, in the case of a flat. In order to claim this right there is also a residence

qualification to fulfill. The tenant, or the tenants spouse must have been resident as a secure tenant (not necessarily in the same property) for two years prior to the application to buy.

The price of the property will be subject to a substantial discount in recognition of the length of time that the tenant has been resident there. Every house purchase is subject to a minimum discount of 32% of the open market value increasing by a further 12% for each year of residence, up to a maximum of 60%. A flat purchase is subject to a minimum 44% discount with 2% per year up to a maximum of 70%.

If the property is sold within three years of purchase then some or all of the discount must be repaid to the local authority or other selling body.

Rights to succeed to a secure tenancy
The tenancy does not end with the death of a secure tenant. If there is a spouse then he/she will succeed to the tenancy subject to having been resident for 1 year, occupying as an only or principal home, prior to the application to succeed.

The courts have held that only persons of the opposite sex can be defined as spouse. However, this ruling may certainly be challenged in the European Court of Human Rights.

Where there is no spouse as defined then a member of the family can succeed, again with the residence qualification in place. If a family cannot decide who should succeed then the local authority or body granting the secure tenancy can make a final decision.

Only one succession is allowed and, on the death of the successor, the local authority can terminate the tenancy through formal procedures and re-let to whom it wishes.

Right to repair and to make improvements
Secure tenants have a right to carry out their own repairs, to make improvements, subject to the landlords consent and also the right to compensation if repairs are not carried out within a set timescale. In general, a secure tenancy is a stronger form of tenure than an assured

tenancy. However, although housing associations grant secure tenancies in certain circumstances, in the main these tenancies are only granted by Local Authorities.

A secure tenancy, like an assured tenancy, can only be brought to an end by a court. There are 17 Grounds for possession in the 1985 Housing Act. However, unlike the assured tenancy, where all grounds are mandatory, all 17 grounds in the secure tenancy are discretionary. Many of these grounds reflect the grounds in the 1988 Housing Act. For a tenancy to be brought to an end, a notice of seeking possession must be served and an application to court made, in the same way as with an assured tenant.

Introductory tenancies

The 1996 Housing Act allowed local housing authorities to elect to set up an introductory tenancy scheme – an election that can be revoked at any time. If the local authority has decided to embark on the policy of adopting introductory tenancies then any tenancy that would be otherwise secure will be an introductory tenancy for a period of one year. In effect this is a period of probation and was introduced to tighten up on the overall behaviour of some of the worst offenders who take up local authority tenancies.

Housing Association tenants

Housing associations are now one of the major providers of affordable housing in the country. Many housing associations are registered with the Housing Corporation, and are known as Registered Social Landlords (RSL's). In order to receive public funding, a housing association has to be registered as an RSL.

Many housing associations now grant a variety of tenancies, assured, assured shorthold, licences and also develop leasehold property. The relevant housing acts will apply to these tenancy types,. However, because of the Housing Corporations monitoring and regulatory function, the assured tenancy issued by a housing association will be significantly stronger than assured tenancies in the private sector.

All tenancies granted after January 15th 1989, by housing associations, will be assured tenancies. Those granted before will be secure tenancies. If a secure tenant transfers to a property occupied by an assured tenant they will lose their secure tenancy. Likewise, the person transferring into a secure tenancy will take on that tenancy.

The assured tenant of a housing association has much the same rights of a secure tenant, passed to them contractually as a result of the Housing Corporations tenants Charter. The only exceptions are the right to buy and a difference in how rents are set.

Many housing associations have, since 1988 taken transfer of local authority property. These large-scale 'stock transfers' have resulted in local authorities housing powers being diminished and those of housing associations enhanced. In this case, the tenancy agreements of local authority tenants will become assured but with a preserved right to buy.

11

PRIVATE TENANCIES IN SCOTLAND

The law governing the relationship between private landlords and tenants in Scotland is different to that in England. Since the beginning of 1989, new private sector tenancies in Scotland have been covered by the Housing (Scotland) Act 1988. Following the passage of this Act, private sector tenants no longer have any protection as far as rent levels are concerned and tenants enjoy less security of tenure.

There are four essential elements in the creation of a tenancy under Scottish law:

- An agreement between landlord and tenant
- The payment of rent. If someone is allowed to occupy a property without an agreement then this will not amount to a tenancy
- A fixed permission date (called an 'ish')
- Possession

The agreement must be in writing if the tenancy is for a period of 1 year or more. Agreements of less than a year can be oral.

Protected tenancies
Before 1989, most private sector tenancies were likely to be protected tenancies. A protected tenancy is a contractual tenancy covered by the Rent Act (Scotland) 1984 and must satisfy the following requirements:

- The house must be let as a dwelling house (this can apply to a house or part of a house)

- The house must be a separate dwelling
- The ratable value must be less than a specified sum

Various categories of dwellings did not qualify as protected tenancies. A protected tenancy retains its status until the death of a tenant or his spouse, or any eligible successor, and therefore some protected tenancies are still in existence today.

Grounds for possession

As is the case in England and Wales, where there is no protected tenancy, the landlord may possess a property only by obtaining a court order. The landlord must serve a notice to quit, giving 28 days notice. A ground for possession must be shown, either discretionary or mandatory before possession can be given.

The grounds for possession are similar to those in England and Wales, with ten mandatory and ten discretionary grounds applying.

Fair rent system

A fair rent system, similar to England and Wales, exists in Scotland for protected tenants. There is a set procedure to be followed, with either the landlord or tenant, or jointly, making an application to the rent officer. Once fixed, the rent is valid for three years. A fresh application can be made within three years if circumstances relating to the tenancy radically alter, such as a substantial refurbishment.

Assured tenants

Under the Housing (Scotland) Act 1988, the assured tenancy was introduced into Scotland coming into force after 2nd January 1989. This is very similar indeed to the assured tenancy introduced into England and Wales in 1989.

A Scottish assured tenancy has three elements:

- the tenancy must be of a house or flat or self contained dwelling. For an agreement to exist, there must be an agreement, rent payable a termination date and possession, as there is in all leases in Scotland

- The house must be let as a separate dwelling. A tenancy may be of a flat, part of a house, or even a single room, provided it is possible for the tenant to carry on all 'the major activities of residential life there, i.e. sleeping, cooking and feeding.
- The tenant must be an individual. A company cannot be given an assured tenancy

The list of exclusions from assured tenancy status are the same as those in England and all the other provisions concerning rent, sub-letting succession, security of tenure and so on, apply.

The grounds for possession and the law governing termination of tenancies is a reflection of English Law.

Short assured tenancies

The Housing Act (Scotland) also introduced 'short assured tenancies', a distinct form of assured tenancy for a fixed term of six months. Again, this is a reflection of the assured shorthold with the same provisions applying.

The Private Tenant 2. The leaseholder

12

THE LAW AND OWNER OCCUPIERS FREEHOLD AND LEASEHOLD

Commonhold and Leasehold Reform Act 2002

The Commonhold and Leasehold Reform Act 2002 introduces into English law an entirely new form of tenure, namely commonhold. It is specifically targeted at blocks of flats, where leasehold has been the normal form of tenure until now.

The Government hopes that commonhold will avoid the tensions and conflicts that have sometimes arisen between leaseholders and freeholders. Time will tell whether that hope will be realised. If it is, doubtless commonhold will come to supersede leasehold as the normal form of tenure for premises divided into flats. For the present, however, commonhold and leasehold regimes will operate side by side, with leasehold predominating.

But it would be very reasonable for a flat owner to say at this point, "Wait a minute. Commonhold has been brought in as an alternative to leasehold; but what was wrong with leasehold? And why do I have to trouble myself with all this anyway? Why can't I simply own my flat, the same way as other people own their houses?"

This is a very fair question. To answer it, we need to look at how the law regards property ownership.

Freehold and Leasehold

The law does not look at property in the same way as most lay people. Most people think in terms of houses and other buildings; the law is more interested in the land beneath. A freehold home owner will say "I own my house." But the law will say "He owns the land on which is built the house he lives in." To the law, the key point is that he owns the land - the buildings on it are incidental.

For practical purposes, the strongest form of title to land is that of freeholder. Freehold title lasts forever; it may be bought and sold, or passed by inheritance. In short, freehold title is tantamount to outright ownership, and is taken as such for the purposes of this book.

Freeholders may, of course, use their land for their own purposes. The freehold home owner is merely the most familiar example. But they may also, if they wish, allow other people to use their land. And this is where leases, and other forms of tenure, come in.

Suppose you would like to make use of a piece of land owned by someone else. The owner is unwilling to sell it to you, but, having no immediate use for it himself, is willing to allow you to use it for a time, perhaps in exchange for payment. At its simplest, this arrangement implies no more than a licence - the owner's (i.e. landlord's) permission for you to be on his land.

But such a licence can be revoked by the landlord at any time, with or without a good reason. As such it is not very valuable, so if the owner wants to make money by allowing other people to use his land, he needs to give them a legal status that they will be willing to pay for. This is achieved by granting a lease or tenancy. It should be noted here that, from the legal point of view, a lease and a tenancy are the same thing; but in practice, the terms tend to be used in different contexts. This is explained below: for the present, we shall call it a lease.

A lease grants the leaseholder permission to use the land for a certain period, which can be anything from a day or two to several thousand years. It will usually attach conditions, for example that the leaseholder must pay rent (usually a sum of money, although in principle other goods or services could constitute rent).

The lease may, but does not have to, put certain restrictions on what the leaseholder may do with the land. But it must, in order to be a lease rather than merely a licence, grant the leaseholder 'exclusive possession'. This is the right to exclude other people, especially the landlord, from the land. Such a right need not be absolute, and exceptions to it are explained later in the book: but it is enough to give the leaseholder a high degree of control over the land, which has become, for the duration of the lease, very much the leaseholder's land rather than the freeholder's. A lease, unless it contains a stipulation to the contrary, may be bought, sold, or inherited; if this happens, all the rights and duties under it pass to the new owner.

Leases and Tenancies

Confusion is often caused by the fact that, although the terms leaseholder (or lessee) and tenant are legally interchangeable, they tend to be used in different senses. The tendency is to refer to short leases as tenancies: the more substantial the rights conferred, and the longer the period for which they run, the likelier it is that the agreement will be referred to as a lease. For the purposes of this book, an agreement will be referred to as a 'tenancy' if it is periodic or runs for a fixed term of less than seven years. A fixed term agreement running for more than seven years will be referred to as a 'lease'.

A 'periodic' tenancy is one that runs from period to period (usually, from week to week or month to month) until something intervenes to stop it, and is conditional on payment of rent. A tenancy that runs for a fixed term of less than seven years has a definite date of expiry but is otherwise similar to a periodic tenancy and will depend on regular payment of rent. Tenancies granted by local authorities and housing associations tend to be periodic; private landlords generally grant either periodic tenancies or short fixed-term tenancies (typically, six months). At any rate, the landlord of a periodic or short-term tenancy will usually accept most of the responsibility for maintaining the property and will charge a relatively high rent to allow for this. If the tenancy is for residential property, the landlord's duty to maintain the dwelling is imposed by law (Landlord and Tenant Act 1985).

It is common for private landlords to insist on prepayment of rent or a deposit before granting a tenancy, and many landlords will levy a separate service charge to cover the cost of some activities that are peripheral to the central one of providing housing; but despite these costs it would be true to say that the principal financial responsibility accepted by a periodic or short-term tenant is that of paying the rent. The position of a leaseholder is very different. The major financial commitment will usually be a substantial initial payment either to the landlord (if the lease is newly created) or to the previous leaseholder. There is still a rent, called a ground rent, payable to the landlord, but it is usually a notional amount (£50 or £100 a year is not uncommon). Its purpose is not so much to give the landlord an income as to give the leaseholder an annual reminder that ultimate ownership of the land is not his.

Types of Leasehold Property

In the context of residential property, it should be noted that the great majority of leases relate to flats rather than houses. This is because of the legal concept of land tenure as described above. If a builder buys some freehold land and covers it in houses, it is possible to parcel out the area so that each bit of freehold land, and the house standing on it, can be sold separately. It does not matter if the houses are semi-detached or terraced, because there is well-established law governing party walls of adjoining freeholders. But if there are flats, the builder has a problem: how can the flats be sold since they cannot be said to stand on separate and distinct bits of land? The answer is to sell leases.

Where flats are sold, each purchaser acquires a lease that gives him specified rights over the parcel of land on which the flats stand. These rights, of course, are shared by the leaseholders of the other flats. In addition, however, each leaseholder gains the right to exclusive possession of part of the building occupying the land - his own flat. The leaseholder would say "I own my flat", but the law says "He owns a lease granting him certain rights, in particular that of access, to a defined parcel of land and the right of exclusive possession of specified parts of a building erected on that land."

This may seem a slightly unusual way of looking at it, but it is fundamental to understanding the way that the law sees the relationship

The Law and owner Occupiers

between leaseholders of flats and their freeholders.

The freehold of flatted property will often be retained by the developer, although sometimes it will be sold to a property company. Formerly, it was common practice for the freehold to be retained even when separate houses were built. This allowed the freeholder to retain an interest in the property and, above all, to regain full possession of it when the lease expired. However, the position of freeholders has been weakened by three key pieces of legislation, the Leasehold Reform Act 1967, the Leasehold Reform, Housing and Urban Development Act 1993, and the Commonhold and Leasehold Reform Act 2002. These Acts are described in detail in Chapter Four: their overall effect is to entitle leaseholders either to the freehold of houses or to a new lease of flats. In view of the legislation, there is now little point in the original owner's attempting to retain the freehold of land on which houses have been built. The exception is where a house is sold on the basis of shared ownership - see below.

Most residential leasehold property therefore consists of flats. Of these, most are in the private sector, comprising purpose-built blocks and (especially in London) conversions of what were once large single houses. The freehold will usually belong to the developer, to a property company, or sometimes to the original owner of the site.

House leases normally give most of the repairing responsibility to the leaseholder - services provided by the freeholder, and therefore service charges, are minimal. In flats, however, although the leaseholder will normally be responsible for the interior of the flat, the freeholder will maintain the fabric of the building and will recoup the costs of doing so by levying service charges on the leaseholders. This is an area of such potential conflict between leaseholders and freeholders that it has been the subject of legislation. It is dealt with fully in Chapter Three.

Mixed-tenure blocks: the right to buy

The general shift from renting to owning means that sometimes flats have been sold in blocks that were originally developed for letting to tenants: the result is often a 'mixed-tenure' block, with both leaseholders and tenants. Although this sometimes happens in the private sector, it is particularly common in blocks owned by local authorities and housing associations, for it is to these that the statutory right to buy applies. This right was created by the Housing Act 1980 and allows most local authority tenants, and some housing association tenants, to buy their homes at a heavily discounted price. Tenants of houses are normally sold the freehold, but tenants of flats become leaseholders.

The right to buy, often seen as the flagship policy of Margaret Thatcher's government, was bitterly opposed, because of the loss it involves of homes otherwise available for letting to the needy and because its popularity with council tenants called into question their previously solid electoral support for Labour. On both counts, its critics' fears have to some extent been realised; however, the right to buy has become an increasingly accepted feature of local authority housing. More recently, a similar but less generous scheme has been introduced covering many housing association tenants not already qualifying for the full right to buy. Purchasing a council home has been, for most of the million or so that have done so, a very satisfactory investment. A minority of purchasers have, however, met with serious difficulties, particularly where they have become leaseholders in mixed tenure blocks of flats: Chapter Three looks at some of the problems affecting management and service charges.

Shared ownership

Another result of the trend towards home ownership has been the dramatic expansion of shared ownership. This is a form of tenure that combines leasing and renting. However, the term 'shared ownership' is something of a misnomer because ownership is not, in fact, shared between the leaseholder and the freeholder. The lease relates to the whole property, not part of it, and the shared owner is as entitled as any other leaseholder to consider himself the owner of his house. The key point about shared ownership leases is not that they give an inferior form of tenure to other leases but that they have different conditions attached. The leaseholder pays less than the full value of the lease; typically, half. In exchange for this concession, he pays not the normal notional ground rent but a much more substantial rent. However, he is much more a leaseholder than he is a tenant, and, like other leaseholders (but unlike tenants) is responsible for the internal repair of the property and, in the case of houses, usually the fabric of the building too.

Shared owners usually have the right to increase their stake as and when they can afford it: this is called 'staircasing' because the owner's share goes up in steps. If the property is a house, the freehold will normally be transferred when the owner's share reaches 100%, and he will then be in the same position as any other freehold home owner. If it is a flat, he will continue to be a leaseholder but there will no longer be a rental (other than ground rent).

Head Leases and Subleases

For the sake of clarity and brevity, this book has been written throughout on the basis that there are only two parties involved: the freeholder and the leaseholder. Usually this picture is accurate; but it is the right of the leaseholder, unless the lease specifically forbids it, to sublet the property, or part of it, to someone else. This means that the leaseholder delegates some of his rights over the property to another person. Obviously, he cannot delegate rights greater than his own, so that if he holds a lease of the property running until 2025 he cannot grant a sublease running until 2050. And he cannot grant a sublease of the whole of his rights because this would leave him with no interest in the property: it would, in fact, amount to the same as an assignment So it is necessary for a sublease that the original leaseholder be left with something; either some period of time or some part of the property.

It is possible in theory to have a whole hierarchy of leases applying to a particular property, starting with the freehold, then the head lease, then a sublease, followed by sub-subleases and possibly sub-sub-subleases below those. There are two rules that limit this kind of proliferation: one, explained above, is that each lease must confer less, in space or time or both, than the one above it; and the other, that if a lease may not be held by the same person as hold the lease (or freehold) immediately above it.

Even with these limitations, however, long chains of ownership can develop. Suppose I own the freehold of a certain piece of land. I am unwilling to sell it outright but I agree to lease it for 125 years to a property developer to build flats, so he becomes the head leaseholder and leases the flats for 99 years to individual subleaseholders. One of these leases his flat for 25 years to someone that, in turn, lets it on a tenancy. The tenant then sublets to some other person who (remembering that tenancies and leases are legally the same) thus becomes a sub-sub-sub-subleaseholder (if I have counted correctly). And it is possible to devise even taller hierarchies of lease than this, provided always that no one holds a lease from himself and that each lease grants less, even if only slightly, than the one above it.

Commonhold

To try to deal with problems arising from the relationship between freeholders and leaseholders, a new form of tenure, 'commonhold', was created by the Commonhold and Leasehold Reform Act 2002. It is designed specifically for use in blocks of flats, and the idea is that all the individual flat owners (or 'unit holders', as the Act calls them) will belong to a 'commonhold association', a registered company that operate under a constitution (the 'memorandum and articles') and act in accordance with a 'commonhold community statement'.

This arrangement ensures that each unit holder will have two separate interests in relation to the property: individually, in his own particular unit, and collectively, in the block as a whole.

13

OBLIGATIONS OF FREEHOLDER AND LEASEHOLDER

General Principles

For centuries the law did little to regulate the relationship between freeholders and leaseholders. The view was taken that they had entered into the relationship of their own free will, and it was up to them to agree whatever terms and conditions they liked. If either party did not keep the bargain, he could of course be sued in the courts, but, on the whole, the law did not interfere in the bargain itself.

In the twentieth century, however, the view grew up that some types of bargain are inherently unfair and even those that are not might still be open to exploitation.

An example of the first type is an agreement that residential property will revert to the original freeholder at the end of a long lease. This meant that when 99-year leases expired, leaseholders found that their homes had abruptly returned to the outright ownership of the heir of the original freeholder, leaving them as mere trespassers liable to be ejected at any time. In practice, freeholders were usually willing to grant a fresh lease, but sometimes only at a very high price that the leaseholder might well be unable to afford. In some cases, freeholders insisted on reclaiming the property however much the leaseholder offered, and the law supported them. This is the state of affairs that led to legislation entitling almost all residential leaseholders to extend their leases, and many of them to claim the freehold. This is dealt with in Chapter Four.

The freeholder's right to demand a service charge is an example of an arrangement that is fair in principle but open to abuse in practice. It is inevitable, especially in flats, that responsibility for some types of repair cannot be ascribed to any individual leaseholder and must therefore be retained by the freeholder; who must, in turn, recoup the cost from leaseholders. However, some freeholders abused this system by levying extravagant service charges that made the service charge a source of profit. To prevent this, there is now a substantial body of legislation designed to ensure that freeholders carry out only the works that are really necessary and that they recover their legitimate costs and no more. The complicated rules governing this are chiefly found in the Landlord and Tenant Act 1985 (as amended) and are described in Chapter Three.

Under the Landlord and Tenant Act 1987, either party to a long lease (one originally granted for at least 21 years) may go to the Leasehold Valuation Tribunal (or 'LVT') to argue that the lease is deficient in some way and needs to be changed. If only the one lease is affected, the tribunal may vary it. Sometimes, however, a number of leases may need to be changed; in this case either the freeholder or 75% of the leaseholders may apply.

Obligations of Leaseholders

The obligations of leaseholders are set out in the lease; indeed, since it is a document drafted by or on behalf of freeholders, one of its main aims is to tell leaseholders what they must and must not do. However, legislation and judicial decisions sometimes come to the leaseholder's assistance.

Consumer legislation can also apply to leases; in particular, the Unfair Terms in Consumer Contracts Regulations 1999 (which replace earlier regulations made in 1995) have a major impact. These apply to standard terms in contracts. This means they normally cover the terms of leases, which are usually presented to potential leaseholders as a package with no opportunity to renegotiate individual terms. Occasionally, however, individual terms can be specifically negotiated and it should be noted that in that case the Unfair Terms Regulations do not apply. Nor will they apply to any lease granted before the earlier version of the regulations came in in July 1995. The Office of Fair Trading has issued advice about the types of term that are likely to be judged unfair in the context of assured tenancies. The OFT has not issued advice about long leases, but it is likely that similar standards would apply.

a: Plain and intelligible language
Over many years property lawyers have developed an obscure and technical language that can have the effect of excluding outsiders. This form of 'legalese' is characterised by unwieldy sentences with few (or no) commas to break them up, long lists often consisting of different names for the same thing, and a vocabulary of unfamiliar words and (worst of all) familiar words given unfamiliar meanings.

For instance, in normal English the verb 'determine' means 'ascertain' or 'firmly decide', but when a property lawyer applies it to a lease it means 'end' or 'terminate' (as in 'the lease shall determine if…'). Property lawyers also have a well-merited reputation for using words like 'hereinafter' and 'aforesaid', which, although not ambiguous, are hardly everyday English, while occasional outbreaks of Latin are not unknown (*pari passu* and *mutatis mutandis*).

Thankfully, this style is going out of fashion and an increasing number of modern leases are being written in more intelligible language, and for leases made since 1995 the Unfair Terms Regulations mean that arcanely written terms may be unenforceable. However, a huge number of leases written in traditional style still have decades or even centuries to run, so unfortunately property lawyers' English will be with us for a long time yet.

b: Terms Unfair on Consumers
There are some terms to which the Office of Fair Trading objects in any consumer contract. These are terms that place an unreasonable burden on the customer (the leaseholder) or give an unfair advantage to the supplier (the freeholder). Some of these terms are common in long leases

There may be a clause in which the leaseholder declares that he has 'read and understood' the lease, even though the document is long and complex and it unlikely that anyone would read (or understand) the whole of it. The aim is to put the leaseholder at a disadvantage in any dispute by arguing that he was fully aware of all the terms of the lease. Another way of loading the scales is a clause allowing the freeholder the final decision about vital matters, such as whether or not the freeholder and the leaseholder have fulfilled their respective obligations under the lease.

These clauses are probably unenforceable in leases made since July 1995, but in earlier leases they are probably valid.

There are other types of clause that are potentially a problem for the leaseholder. An example is a clause laying down procedural formalities. Such a clause is not necessarily a problem: for instance, leases commonly require formal communications between the freeholder and the leaseholder to be in writing, and this is a perfectly reasonable requirement because it reduces the chances misunderstandings or disputes about who said what. But it is harder to justify a requirement for notices to be sent by registered post, and some leases stipulate procedures that are so onerous that the aim seems to be to deter leaseholders from exercising their rights.

Similar comments apply to clauses imposing financial penalties for breaches of the lease. This is not necessarily unreasonable, but sometimes the penalties are out of all proportion to the nature of the breach.

Some leases require the leaseholder to join with the freeholder (and help with the cost) in responding to legal or other notices pertaining to the property. Again, this may be reasonable in some circumstances, but as a blanket requirement it can act against leaseholders' interests.

An interesting and debatable issue is the prohibition of set-off, which is a standard clause in most leases. 'Set-off' is the practice of deducting (or 'setting off') from any payment made by one party under an agreement any sums that are owed by the other party. For instance, suppose a leaseholder considers that a repair to the fabric of the building is the freeholder's responsibility, but the freeholder either disputes this or fails to take any action. Eventually the leaseholder does the work at his own expense, and next time the annual service charge falls due he reimburses himself by deducting, or 'setting off', the cost from his service charge payment.

Leaseholders like set-off because it is an easy way of reclaiming disputed sums from the freeholder, and it shifts onto the freeholder the onus of continuing the dispute. Freeholders dislike it for exactly the same reasons, which is why leases normally prohibit it. The Office of Fair Trading, in its advice on assured tenancies, says that prohibiting set-off is unfair, but it is not clear whether the same advice would apply to leases.

The possibility that unfair, or potentially unfair, clauses will feature in a lease underlines the need for competent legal advice before signing it. An experienced solicitor will be able to advise whether doubtful clauses can be, or are likely to be, used against leaseholders. Leaseholders may also have remedies available under the Landlord and Tenant Act: this is covered below and, in the key area of service charges, in the next Chapter.

c: Restrictive clauses in leases
So far, we have looked at leases as if they were consumer contracts, and outlined some of the clauses they may contain that could affect leaseholders in their capacity as consumers. But there are some further potentially difficult terms that relate specifically to property issues. These terms are not necessarily unreasonable. For example, in a lease concerning an upstairs flat it would be quite normal to have a clause requiring the leaseholder to keep the premises carpeted. This makes sense because bare floors, although currently very fashionable, could be very noisy for the people in the flat below.

The Office of Fair Trading's advice identifies several types of sweeping provisions that would, if they were enforced, considerably restrict the tenant's ability to live a normal life. Although the OFT's advice relates to assured tenancies, similar objections would probably apply to these clauses in leases. For example:

- **Pets** Leases often lay down that the leaseholder may not own pets, or may not do so without the freeholder's permission.

- **Upkeep** Leases may say that the leaseholder must decorate periodically - say, every five or seven years. Where there is a garden, it is common for the leascholder to be required to keep it in good order.

- **Business** Leases often lay down that the leaseholder must not run any sort of business from his home.

- **Use as residence** A lease will generally say that the property is to be used for the residential purposes of the leaseholder and his household, and that it cannot be sublet. It will sometimes attempt to restrict how many people may live there apart from the leaseholder.

- **Other** Leases sometimes forbid such things as the keeping of flammable materials and the installation of television aerials or satellite dishes. They may require leaseholders to drain hot water systems whenever they are away, or keep the premises clean and free of dust.

It is easy to see why freeholders want such clauses in the lease: it is because they realise that there will be serious problems if someone attempts, for instance, to keep four alsatians in a studio flat. The neighbours will be inconvenienced and will complain to the freeholder, and leases of other flats in the same block will become difficult to sell.

The same arguments could apply if one of the leaseholders allows his flat to fall into complete decorative decay or if he runs a noisy and busy trade from his home.

But the kind of blanket rules that appear in many leases go too far. A rule against any pets at all forbids not only four noisy alsatians but also entirely inoffensive pets such as a budgie or a goldfish. In the same way, prohibiting business activities means that the leaseholder may not use his home to write a book for publication, or address envelopes, and so on - types of homeworking that could not possibly inconvenience anyone.

The rule against sub-letting also prevents leaseholders from exploiting the value of their property by letting it out, something that is open to most home-owners and is increasingly accepted as normal.

For leases made since July 1995, these sweeping clauses are probably unfair and unenforceable. But even for older leases, the reality is that such broad provisions are seldom enforced. Freeholders, and their lawyers, like them because they feel that they preserve their freedom of action, allowing them to decide whether or not to enforce the lease if it is clear that one of these blanket conditions is being broken. But there are two problems with this attitude.

The first is that it creates uncertainty in the minds of leaseholders. Suppose the leases in a block of flats prohibit all pets, but leaseholder A has a goldfish and no action has been taken even though the freeholder is aware of the infringement. Leaseholder B may well conclude that there will be no objection if he gets a cat. If still there is no action, leaseholder C may feel able to get a couple of dogs - and so on. So the fact that restrictions are so broad can have the paradoxical effect of reducing their effectiveness.

The second problem is that if, in the example just given, the freeholder takes legal action to force C to get rid of the dogs, it is possible that C will argue in court that the treatment of the other leaseholders shows that the freeholder is not seriously interested in banning pets and that the action has been motivated rather by petty spite or bias.

It would be better if freeholders and their lawyers drafted leases that say what they mean: not that leaseholders may have no pets at all, but that they may have no pets apt to damage the property or cause inconvenience or annoyance to other persons. The same principle should apply to clauses dealing with sub-letting or working from home.

It is unfortunate that this book is forced to advise leaseholders to ignore some parts of their leases. The responsibility for this, however, lies with freeholders and their lawyers for writing into standard leases blanket conditions purporting to prohibit entirely inoffensive behaviour. This practice makes it inevitable, in the real world, that leaseholders will disregard certain clauses, and that books like this will have to give them some indication of when they can probably do so safely. Most leaseholders exercise common sense and realise that the freeholder is unlikely to take action unless there is a complaint, which means that the leaseholder may do almost whatever he pleases provided he refrains from provoking anyone. It is sensible to stay on good terms with neighbours to ensure that if anything is bothering them they take it up directly with you rather than report the matter to the freeholder. Other leaseholders will also be able to tell you what view has been taken in the past - both by other residents and by the freeholder - in doubtful cases.

d: Restrictions on sale
Some leases restrict the kind of person to whom the lease may be sold (or 'assigned' - see below). For example, a housing scheme may have been intended specifically for the elderly. Clearly, it will not be maintained as such if leaseholders are free to assign or bequeath their leases to whomever they please, so the lease will say that it may be assigned only to persons above a certain age, and that if it is inherited by anyone outside the age group it must be sold on to someone qualified to hold it. Although this could be described as an onerous term because it makes it more difficult to find a buyer and may reduce the lease's value, it is reasonable given the need to ensure that the scheme continues to house elderly people exclusively. And the restriction it imposes is not too severe because so many potential purchasers qualify.

However, some leases define much more narrowly to whom they may be sold. Sometimes the freeholder is a body owned and run by the leaseholders themselves, and in these cases it is usual to require that all leaseholders must join the organisation and, if they leave it, must immediately dispose of the lease to someone that is willing to join.

Again, such a term is not necessarily unacceptable. If the organisation makes relatively light demands on its members (perhaps no more than a modest admission fee or annual subscription), the restriction is unlikely greatly to diminish the value of the lease. If, however, the organisation expects much more from its members - perhaps that they actively take part in running it, or that they pay a large annual subscription - the value of the lease will be severely reduced because it will be difficult to find purchasers willing to accept the conditions. A key point is whether the organisation has power to expel members, thus forcing them to sell; and, if so, in what circumstances and by whom this power can be exercised.

e: Access

Virtually any lease will contain a clause allowing the freeholder to enter the property in order to inspect or repair it. This has the effect of qualifying the leaseholder's right of exclusive possession (see below), but only subject to certain conditions. The freeholder (or the freeholder's servants, such as agents or contractors) may enter only at reasonable times, and subject to the giving of reasonable notice. If these conditions are not met, the leaseholder is under no obligation to allow them in; and, even when the conditions are met, the landlord will be trespassing if he enters the property without the leaseholder's consent. If the leaseholder refuses consent even though the time is reasonable and reasonable notice has been given, the landlord's remedy is to get a court order against the leaseholder compelling him to grant entry. It is probable, in such a case, that the landlord will seek, and get, an award of legal costs against the leaseholder.

f: Arbitration

Many leases contain clauses providing that disputes can be submitted to arbitration at the request of either party. By the Commonhold and Leasehold Reform Act, the effect of these clauses is limited, because the results will not be binding so far as the Leasehold Valuation Tribunal is concerned. If, however, once a dispute has arisen, the parties to agree to submit it to an agreed arbitrator, they are bound by the result, which is enforceable by the courts. If such a 'post-dispute' arbitration finds that the leaseholder is in breach, this is equivalent to a finding by the LVT and will (if the other requirements are met) allow the freeholder to proceed with forfeiture. Arbitration may be a useful mechanism in some cases, and it may be cheaper and quicker than legal action, but it may be difficult to find an arbitrator in whom both parties have confidence.

Obligations of Freeholders
a: Exclusive possession and quiet enjoyment
The first and most important obligation on the freeholder, without which there would be no legal lease at all, is to respect the leaseholder's rights of 'exclusive possession' and 'quiet enjoyment'. Exclusive possession has been explained in Chapter One as the right to occupy the property and exclude others from it, especially the freeholder. Quiet enjoyment is another way of underlining the leaseholder's rights over the property: it means that the freeholder may not interfere with the leaseholder's use of the property provided that the terms of the lease are observed.

However, the leaseholder's right to quiet enjoyment applies only to breaches by the freeholder or the freeholder's servants such as agents or contractors. It is important to note this because the term is sometimes thought to mean that the freeholder must protect the leaseholder against any activity by anyone that interferes with his use of the property: this is not so. For example, if the freeholder carries out some activity elsewhere in the building that interferes with the leaseholder, the leaseholder's right to quiet enjoyment has been breached and he is entitled to redress unless the freeholder can show that the activity was necessary, for instance to comply with repairing obligations under the lease. But if the interference is caused by someone else, perhaps another leaseholder, the freeholder's obligation to provide quiet enjoyment has not been breached. And it is worth stressing in this connection that even if the other leaseholder is in breach of his lease, it is entirely up to the freeholder whether or not to take action: other leaseholders have no power to force the freeholder to deal with the situation.

This means that if one leaseholder is breaking his lease by holding noisy parties late at night, the other leaseholders may ask, but may not require, the freeholder to take action to enforce the lease. They may, however, take legal action directly against the offending leaseholder for nuisance.

b: The 'section 48' notice

Another important protection for leaseholders is found in section 48 of the Landlord and Tenant Act 1987. This was designed to deal with the situation in which freeholders seek to avoid their responsibilities by (to put it bluntly) doing a disappearing act. Sometimes freeholders would provide no address or telephone number or other means of contact, meaning that leaseholders were unable to hold the freeholder to his side of the agreement. Sections 47 and 48 therefore lay down that the freeholder must formally notify the leaseholder of his name and give an address within England and Wales at which he can be contacted, and that this information must be repeated on every demand for rent or service charge. This has proved especially valuable for leaseholders where the freeholder lives abroad, or is a company based abroad. It should be noted that the address does not have to be the freeholder's home, nor, if the freeholder is a company, its registered office; often it will be the address of a solicitor or property management company, or simply an accommodation address. But the key point is that any notice, or legal writ, is validly served if sent to that address, and the freeholder is not allowed to claim that it never came to his notice.

It is not necessary for the notice required by section 48 to be given in a separate document; it is enough if the name and address is clearly given as part of some other document such as a service charge demand. But if the necessary notice is **not** given, no payment of rent, service charge, or anything else is due to the freeholder; the leaseholder may lawfully withhold it until section 48 is complied with. But leaseholders withholding payments on this ground must be careful; once the notice is given, it has retrospective effect, so that all the money due to the freeholder then becomes due immediately. Any leaseholder withholding money on the grounds that section 48 has not been complied with should, therefore, make sure that he has the money easily available so that he can pay up if he has to.

c: Good management

The freeholder is under an obligation to ensure that his management responsibilities are carried out in a proper and appropriate way. Leaseholders can challenge the freeholder in court or at the LVT if they believe they can show that they are not receiving the standard of management to which they are entitled. This may be an expensive and lengthy process but it better than the alternative, sometimes resorted to by leaseholders, of withholding rent or service charge. This is risky because, whatever the shortcomings of the freeholder's management, it puts the leaseholders in breach of the conditions of their lease and, as such, demonstrably in the wrong (even if the freeholder may be in the wrong as well).

Withholding due payments is therefore not recommended unless the freeholder is so clearly at fault that arguably no payment is due - for instance, if the service being charged for has clearly not been provided at all (as opposed to being provided inadequately), or if there has been no 'section 48' notice (see above). If leaseholders choose to withhold payment, they are strongly advised to keep the money readily to hand so that they can pay up at once if the freeholder rectifies the problem; the danger otherwise is that they will be taken to court and required to pay immediately to avoid forfeiture (see below).

Powers of Leaseholders over Management

If leaseholders want a scrutiny of the standards of management of their flats, they have power under the Leasehold Reform, Housing and Urban Development Act 1993 to demand a management audit by an auditor acting on behalf of at least two-thirds of the qualifying leaseholders. Qualifying leaseholders are those with leases of residential property originally granted for 21 years or more and requiring them to contribute to the cost of services.

The purpose of the audit, the costs of which must be met by the leaseholders demanding it, is to discover whether the freeholder's duties are being carried out efficiently and effectively. The auditor is appointed by the leaseholders and must be either a qualified accountant or a qualified surveyor and must not live in the block concerned. The auditor has the right to demand papers from the freeholder and can go to court if they are not produced.

Leaseholders' Right to Manage

Leaseholders with long leases (those originally granted for 21 years or more) also have the right to take over management of their block if they wish. This applies to blocks of two or more flats (five or more if there is a resident landlord) and no substantial non-residential part. It does not apply if the freeholder is a local authority.

The leaseholders must first form a 'Right to Manage' company ('RtM' company), which is a limited company whose membership is confined to leaseholders and the freeholder. Before seeking to take over management the RtM company must advise all leaseholders of its intention and invite them to participate. Fourteen days after this invitation, and provided the RtM company includes at least half the eligible tenants (or both, if only two are eligible), it can serve a claim notice on the landlord (or on the Leasehold Valuation Tribunal, if the landlord is untraceable) giving at least four months' notice of its intention to take over the management. The landlord has a month to serve a counter-notice objecting to the claim, in which case the LVT will adjudicate. If no counter-notice is served, or if the LVT so decides, the RtM company duly takes over management.

The landlord must bring to an end as quickly as possible any existing management arrangements applying to the block. The RtM company takes over the landlord's management functions, including services, repairs, maintenance, improvements, and insurance. The landlord retains its role in respect of any flats without long leaseholders (for example, those let on assured tenancies), and continues to deal with forfeiture (for more on forfeiture see the section below 'If the lease is breached'). Essentially the RtM company steps into the landlord's shoes so far as management is concerned, and it is responsible to both the landlord and the individual leaseholders for the proper carrying out of its functions.

Many leases require the landlord's approval before certain things can be done, such as assigning the lease or sub-letting. The RtM company takes over this function from the landlord, but must consult the landlord before granting approval. If the landlord objects, the matter is referred to the LVT. It seems, however, that refusal of consent by the RtM is final and cannot be challenged by the landlord (although it might be challenged by the leaseholder in question on the ground that the relevant term of the lease is unenforceable). The RtM company has authority to enforce covenants in the lease, but not by means of forfeiture.

At first blush the power to take over management in this way may appear attractive. However, leaseholders should think very carefully before they commit themselves; there are some potential snags.

The biggest problem is one of enforcement. So long as all leaseholders are agreed about what needs to be done, and are all willing and able to meet their obligations (including that of paying for services), enforcement will not be an issue and all will be well. But if some individual leaseholders refuse to pay their share, or fail to abide by the covenants in their leases, the RtM company will have to act to enforce the leases and this may well be difficult. In the first place, any steps to enforce leases will pit neighbour against neighbour and are virtually certain to cause animosity in the block. Secondly, the powerful tool of forfeiture, or threatened forfeiture, is denied to a RtM company. Finally, the RtM company, unlike most freeholders, will not have any substantial financial resources that would allow it to pursue lengthy legal action against individual leaseholders.

There are other issues. The RtM company will depend on the voluntary efforts of its members, and experience shows that many people are not willing to put in the time and effort involved in attending meetings and carrying out essential administration. RtM companies have to operate under a special constitution laid down by the Government; the aim of this is to guarantee all leaseholders' rights to be involved, but because the constitution is a standard document applying to all cases it is likely that many leaseholders will find it clumsy and inflexible. Finally, there is the question of continuing relations with the freeholder, which will expect its interests as ultimate owner to be respected by the RtM company.

In short, leaseholders contemplating the formation of a RtM company need to be sure that they are committed not only for the immediate effort of setting it up but for the long haul of carrying out management in the future. They should also recognise that, no matter how united everyone may be to start with, sooner or later the issue of enforcement will rear its head. They should certainly get legal advice about their new responsibilities before committing themselves.

The law allows another remedy in extreme cases of mismanagement. A leaseholder can use the Landlord and Tenant Act 1987 to force the appointment of a managing agent to run the block instead of the freeholder. The leaseholder must serve a notice telling the freeholder what the problems are and warning that unless they are put right a Leasehold Valuation Tribunal will be asked to appoint a managing agent. The LVT may make such an order if it satisfied that it is 'just and convenient'; the Act mentions, as specific examples where this may apply, cases where the freeholder is in breach of obligations under the lease and cases where service charges are being levied in respect of work of a poor standard or an unnecessarily high standard. It should be noted that this procedure, although in some ways it resembles the procedures for collective enfranchisement in Chapter Five, differs from them in that it can be carried out by any individual leaseholder; it does not require the consent of a majority. Note too that the procedure is not available if the freeholder is a local authority, a registered housing association, or the Crown.

Recognised Tenants' Association

A recognised tenants' association (RTA), where there is one, has additional rights to be consulted about managing agents. The RTA can serve a notice requiring the freeholder to supply details of the managing agent and the terms of the management agreement. Recognised tenants' associations are more important, however, in connexion with service charges, so they are explained in the Chapter Three.

Leaseholders that are receiving a consistently poor or overpriced service may also wish to consider getting rid of the freeholder altogether by collective enfranchisement under the Leasehold Reform, Housing and Urban Development Act 1993.

Assignment of Leases

One of the most important characteristics of a lease - in marked contrast to most tenancies - is that it may be bought and sold. Usually, the freeholder has no say in this: the leaseholder may sell to whom he likes for the best price he can get, provided that the purchaser agrees to be bound by the terms of the lease. It is, however, usual for the lease to lay down that the freeholder must be informed of any change of leaseholder.

What actually happens when a lease is sold is that the vendor agrees to transfer to the buyer his rights and obligations under the lease. This is called 'assignment' of the lease. In some types of housing the freeholder has the right to intervene if an assignment is envisaged. The housing may, for instance, be reserved for a particular category of resident, such as the retired, so the freeholder is allowed to refuse consent to the assignment if the purchaser does not qualify.

It was mentioned above that the assignee takes over all the rights and responsibilities attaching to the lease. This means, for instance, that he takes responsibility for any arrears of service charge. This is why purchasers' solicitors go to such lengths to ensure that no arrears or other unusual obligations are outstanding.

If the Lease Is Breached

If the terms of a lease are broken, the party offended against can go to court. This may be the leaseholder, for instance if the freeholder has failed to carry out a repair. But it is normally the freeholder that takes the leaseholder to court, for failure to pay ground rent or service charges or for breach of some other requirement.

It is for the court, if satisfied that the lease has been breached, to decide what to do. The normal remedy will be that the offending party must pay compensation and that the breach (if it is still continuing) must be put right. It is also likely that the loser will be obliged to pay the winner's legal costs as well as his own, a penalty often considerably more severe that the requirement to pay compensation.

A much more severe remedy open to the freeholder if the leaseholder is in breach is forfeiture of the lease. This means what it says: the lease is forfeit to the freeholder. Forfeiture is sometimes threatened by the more aggressive class of freeholder but the good news for leaseholders is that in practice courts have shown themselves loth to grant it except in very serious cases. Since the Housing Act 1996 took effect, forfeiture for unpaid service charges has been made more difficult for freeholders; this is covered in the next Chapter.

Where forfeiture is threatened for any reason other than failure to pay rent (which, depending on the terms of the lease, may or may not include the service charge element), the freeholder must first serve a 'section 146 notice', so called after the relevant provision of the Law of Property Act 1925. In this he must state the nature of the breach of the lease, what action is required to put it right; if he wants monetary compensation for the breach, the notice must state this too.

Before the section 146 notice can be issued, it must be established that a breach of the lease has occurred. If the leaseholder has admitted the breach, the notice can be issued; otherwise, it must have been decided by a court, the LVT, or an independent arbitrator that the leaseholder is in breach. Moreover, the breach of the lease specified in the section 146 notice must have occurred during the twelve years preceding the notice. For breaches older than this, no valid section 146 notice can be served and so forfeiture is not available. If the notice is not complied with, the freeholder may proceed to forfeit; but the leaseholder may go to court for relief from forfeiture. In practice, courts have generally been willing to grant relief, but they cannot do so unless it is formally applied for. If the leaseholder, perhaps failing to realise the seriousness of the situation, fails to go to court and seek relief, the forfeiture will go ahead.

Forfeiture will be considered again in the next Chapter, which covers the special rules applying to forfeiture for failure to pay service charges.

The Government has announced that ultimately it intends to replace forfeiture by a different remedy that will recognise the value of the leaseholder's interest. Until this happens, however, forfeiture remains available and leaseholders must take care to avoid any possibility of its being used against them.

If the freeholder breaches the lease, the leaseholder can go to court and seek an order requiring the freeholder to remedy the breach, to pay damages, or to do both. The commonest type of breach complained of by leaseholders is failure to carry out repairs, and this explains why action by leaseholders is less usual; they know that if they force the freeholder to do repairs the costs will be recovered through service charges. Legal action may be the best course if the dispute affects a single leaseholder; but if a number of leaseholders are involved they may well prefer to get rid of the freeholder altogether by collectively enfranchising their leases as described in Chapter Four.

Leasehold Valuation Tribunals

Several references have already been made to Leasehold Valuation Tribunals. These bodies operate throughout England and Wales. They are appointed jointly by the Lord Chancellor and (in England) the Environment Secretary and (in Wales) the Welsh Secretary. They perform a large number of quasi-judicial functions in relation to property, especially leasehold property, and feature frequently in this book.

14
OWNER OCCUPIERS AND SERVICE CHARGES

The Role of Service Charges
By far the commonest cause of dispute between leaseholders and freeholders is the provision of services and, especially, the levying of service charges. In extreme cases, leaseholders have been asked to contribute thousands of pounds towards the cost of major repairs, and have even suffered forfeiture of the lease if they are unable, or unwilling, to comply. Happily, such instances are rare; but even where the service charges are more moderate, they are often resented by leaseholders. The purpose of this Chapter is to explain the legitimate purpose of service charges and the legal obligations of both the leaseholder and the freeholder, and to offer some warnings about the circumstances where very high service charges are likely to be found.

The difference between long leases and tenancies (short-term and periodic) was set out in Chapter One. One of its most important consequences is that services are paid for in a very different way. In a periodic or short-term tenancy, all the basic costs of providing and managing the housing are paid out of the rent. It is true that there will sometimes be a service charge as well, but it normally covers things such as the provision of heating or communal lighting - things that, however necessary they may be, are peripheral to the central function of providing housing. As a result, service charges in rented property are usually quite moderate and cause little argument.

Contrast the position in leasehold housing. In both types of housing, the landlord is under a legal obligation to the residents to keep the property in good condition and to carry out any work necessary for that purpose; but the landlord of rented property is expected to meet the costs from the rent, whereas the freeholder of leasehold stock has no rent to fall back on (apart from the normally negligible ground rent). How, then, are major costs to be met when they arise? The answer, of course, is from the service charge, which is, therefore, of central importance to the management of leasehold property.

From the freeholder's point of view, the logic of service charges is impeccable. It is perfectly reasonable for freeholders to point out:

* that leaseholders benefit from the work because it has maintained or improved their homes; and
* that the fact that the work has been done means that leaseholders will get a better price when they come to sell; and
* that people that own their homes freehold have to find the money to meet costs of this kind.

To sum up the freeholder's position: the costs have been incurred; the work is for the benefit of the leaseholders; so the leaseholders must pay.

Leaseholders can point out in reply that someone that owns his home freehold can make his own choice when and how to do the repair; he can put up with a slightly leaking roof if he cannot afford to repair it. But freeholders of leasehold property have no such discretion: they are obliged under the lease to do their repairs promptly and if they did not would be liable to legal action by any leaseholder.

So it is difficult for leaseholders to object to the principle of service charges or to ask the freeholder to refrain from carrying out work or to delay it. In short, the purchase of a lease means the acceptance of a commitment to pay the appropriate share of costs.

But does this mean that leaseholders have no scope to challenge or query service charges? No; under sections 18 to 30 of the Landlord and Tenant Act 1985, they have extensive legal protection against improper or unreasonable charging by freeholders, and this is discussed later in the Chapter. First, however, we should look at how a typical service charge is made up.

The Components of a Service Charge

The lease will say how often service charges are levied: typically, six-monthly or annually. It is usual to collect the ground rent at the same time, but this is usually a fairly small component of the bill. The service charge proper will normally consist of three elements.

- **The management fee** is the charge made by the freeholder, or the freeholder's agent, to cover the administrative cost of providing the service and collecting the charge. Usually it will be much the same amount from one year to the next, but if major works have occurred the management fee will usually be higher to cover the extra costs of appointing and supervising contractors; 15% of the cost of the works is a common figure.
- **Direct costs (routine expenditure)** cover costs such as the supply of electricity to communal areas, building insurance, and the like. Again, these costs are likely to be fairly constant from year to year, so leaseholders know in advance roughly how much they are likely to have to pay.

- **Direct costs (exceptional expenditure)** cover costs that are likely to be irregular but heavy. They usually result from maintenance and repair, and it is because this component of the service charge is so unpredictable that it gives rise to so many problems. Where a house has been divided into leasehold flats, the freeholder's costs will usually be similar to what a normal home owner would be obliged to pay; in other words, the costs may well be in the thousands (for a new roof, say) but are unlikely to be higher. Even so, a charge of £5000 for a new roof, albeit divided between three or four flats, is still a major cost from the point of view of the individual leaseholder, especially if it is unexpected. The situation can be far worse in blocks of flats, where the costs of essential repair and maintenance may run into millions. Replacement of worn-out lifts, for example, is notoriously costly; and costs arising from structural defects are likely to be higher still. Suppose it costs £2 million to remove asbestos from a block of forty flats: the average cost per flat is £50 000, a figure that may well exceed the value of the individual flats, and is likely to be beyond the reach of most leaseholders. The problem of exceptionally high service charges is looked at in greater detail at the end of the chapter.

Unreasonable Service Charges
a: General Principles

Sections 18 to 30 of the Landlord and Tenant Act 1985, as amended by subsequent legislation, grant substantial protection to leaseholders of residential property. This protection was introduced after complaints of exploitation by unscrupulous leaseholders, who were alleged to be carrying out unnecessary, or even fictitious, repairs at extravagant prices, whilst not providing the information that would have enabled leaseholders to query the bill. The general effect of the Act is to require freeholders to provide leaseholders with full information about service charges and to consult them before expensive works are carried out. It must be stressed, however, that although the Act protects leaseholders against sharp practice by freeholders, and will prevent the recovery of **unreasonable** costs, it will support freeholders, provided they have gone through the necessary formalities described below, in the recovery of their **reasonable** costs, even if those costs are high. To take the example used above of the removal of asbestos from a block of flats: the fact that the average cost per flat is as high as £50 000 does not, in itself, make the charge unreasonable - to make use of the Act, objecting leaseholders have to show, when they are notified that the work is to be carried out (not when the bills arrive), that it was not necessary or could have been carried out cheaper.

A few leases, namely those granted under the right to buy by local authorities or registered housing associations, have some additional protection under the Housing Act 1985 (see below), but sections 18 to 30 apply to all residential leases where the service charge depends on how much the freeholder spends. They set out the key rules that freeholders must observe in order to recover the cost, including overheads, of 'services, repairs or improvements, maintenance or insurance', as well as the freeholder's costs of management. Sections 18 to 30 only apply to service charges, not to other charges such as ground rent.

It should be noted that failure by leaseholders to pay the service charge does not relieve the freeholder of the obligation to provide the services. The freeholder's remedy is to sue the leaseholder for the outstanding charges, or even to seek forfeiture of the lease (see below).

Section 19 of the Act provides the key protection to leaseholders by laying down that service charges are recoverable only if they are 'reasonably incurred' and if the services or works are of a reasonable standard. This means that the charge:
- must relate to some form of service, repair, maintenance, improvement, or insurance that the freeholder is required to provide under the lease;
- must be reasonable (that is, the landlord may not recover costs incurred unnecessarily or extravagantly);
- may cover overheads and management costs only if these too are reasonable.

In addition, the charge must normally be passed on to the leaseholders within 18 months of being incurred, and in some cases the freeholder must consult leaseholders before spending the money. These points are covered below.

The Housing Act 1996 gave leaseholders new powers to refer service charges to the Leasehold Valuation Tribunal (LVT). This is covered below (*Challenging Service Charges*).

b: Consultation with Leaseholders
Section 20 (as amended by the Commonhold and Leasehold Reform Act 2002) provides extra protection where the cost of works is more than a certain limit, £250 or more to the leaseholder. Costs above this level are irrecoverable unless the freeholder has taken steps to inform

and consult tenants, although there are a exceptions in special cases (see below). If the leaseholders are not represented by a recognised tenants' association (for which see below) these steps are as follows:

> **Estimates** At least two estimates must be obtained, of which at least one must be from someone wholly unconnected from the freeholder (obviously a building firm that the freeholder owns or works for is not 'wholly unconnected'; nor is the freeholder's managing agent. Arguably, even a building firm with which the freeholder has no formal connexion could be 'connected' with him if he gives it so much work that it depends on him and is thus subject to his influence)

> **Notification to leaseholders** The freeholder must either display a copy of the estimates somewhere they are likely to be seen by everyone liable to pay the service charges or preferably send copies to everyone liable to pay the charge

> **Consultation** The notification must describe the works to be carried out and must seek comments and observations, giving a deadline for replies and an address in the UK to which they may be sent. The deadline must be at least a month after the notice was sent or displayed.

> **Freeholder's response** The freeholder must 'have regard' to representations received. This does not mean, of course, that the freeholder must do what the leaseholders say. It does mean, however, that the freeholder must consider any comments received, and good freeholders often demonstrate that they have done so by sending a reasoned reply (i.e. not a form letter or bare acknowledgment, but a letter that responds specifically to any points made), even though the Act does not require them to.

It was mentioned above that there are special cases in which these requirements can be set aside. If a service charge is challenged, it is defence for the freeholder to show that the works were so urgent that there was no time for proper consultation. It is also possible for freeholders to enter into long term agreements to carry out works or provide services over a period of years; if so, they must consult before the agreement is entered into but they need not consult separately before each particular element of expenditure under the agreement. Finally, the LVT has a general power to set aside the usual consultation requirements if it seems fair to do so.

Section 20 is important because it gives the leaseholders notification of any unusual items in the offing and gives them an opportunity to raise any concerns and objections. If the leaseholder has any reservations at all, it is vital that they be put before the freeholder at this stage. It is unlikely, in the event of legal action later, that courts or LVTs will support a leaseholder that raised no objection until the bill arrived.

It is surprisingly common for freeholders and their agents to fail to comply with the requirements of section 20. This comment applies not only where the freehold is owned by an individual or a relatively small organisation (where mistakes might be more understandable) but also where the freeholder is a large, well resourced body like a local authority (which should be well able to understand and carry out its legal duties).

As a result leaseholders are often paying service charges that are not due, so all leaseholders should, before paying a service charge containing unusual items, ensure that section 20, if it applies, has been scrupulously followed. If not, they can refuse to pay.

c: Other Protection for Leaseholders
Grant-aided works: If the freeholder has received a grant towards the cost of carrying out the works, the amount must be deducted from the service charge levied on leaseholders.

Late charging: Service charge bills may not normally include costs incurred more than eighteen months earlier. The freeholder may, however, notify leaseholders within the eighteen-month period that they will have to pay a certain cost, and then bill them later. This may happen if, for instance, the freeholder is in dispute with a contractor about the level of a bill or the standard of work.

Pre-charging: Sometimes a lease will contain a provision allowing the freeholder to make a charge to cover future costs besides those already incurred. This practice, which is perfectly lawful in itself, may be in the interests of the leaseholders by spreading over a longer period the cost of major works. It is, however, subject to the same overall requirement of reasonableness.

Court costs: Section 20C provides protection against a specific abuse of the service charge system by freeholders. Previously, freeholders tended to regard their legal costs as part of the process of managing the housing and thus as recoverable from leaseholders. Such an attitude is not necessarily unreasonable: if, for instance, the freeholder is suing a builder for poor work, he is, in effect, acting on behalf of all the leaseholders and it is fair that they should pay any legal costs. But suppose the freeholder were involved in legal proceedings against one of the leaseholders: if the leaseholder lost, he would probably to be ordered to pay the freeholder's costs as well as his own; but if the freeholder lost, and had to pay both his own and the leaseholder's costs, he could simply, under the previous law, recover the money as part of the management element in the service charge. This meant that the freeholder was able to pursue legal action against leaseholders without fear of heavy legal costs in the event of defeat, the very factor that deters most people from too ready a resort to law. To prevent this, section 20C allows leaseholders to seek an order that the freeholder's legal costs must not be counted towards service charges.

Service charges held on trust: Section 42 of the Landlord and Tenant Act 1987 further strengthened the position of leaseholders by laying

Owner Occupiers and Service Charges

down that the freeholder, or the freeholder's agent, must hold service charge monies in a suitable interest-bearing trust fund that will ensure that the money is protected and cannot be seized by the freeholder's

creditors if the freeholder goes bankrupt or into liquidation. However, public sector freeholders, notably local authorities and registered housing associations, are exempt from this requirement.

Administration charges: These are the freeholder's costs incurred in complying with leaseholders' requests for information and approvals under the terms of the lease. All such charges must be reasonable. Any demand for administration charges must be accompanied by a summary of leaseholders' rights and obligations in relation to them. The LVT has the power to decide whether or not an administration charge is payable, and if so, to whom and by whom together with the amount, date payable and the manner in which it is paid.

Ground rent: Strictly, this is not part of the service charge but as it is usually collected along with it, it is covered here. It will be specified in the lease and is usually a fairly modest annual sum in the order of £50 or £100. Leaseholders should note that, unlike the service charge and most other charges, the ground rent is not intended to compensate the freeholder for any costs or trouble; it is simply a payment by which the leaseholder recognises that ultimately the property belongs to the freeholder. Therefore freeholders are under no obligation to demonstrate that it is reasonable. But it is not payable unless the landlord has issued a formal request for it, which must specify the amount of the payment, the date on which the leaseholder is liable to pay it and the date (if different) on which it would have been payable under the lease. The date for payment must be at least 30 days and not more than 60 days after the date of the notice.

Insurance: Usually, any insurance required under the lease will be taken out by the freeholder and this is discussed below. Occasionally, however, the leaseholder will be required to take out insurance with a company nominated by the freeholder. If the leaseholder thinks he is getting a poor deal, he can apply to the county court or a Leasehold Valuation Tribunal which, if satisfied that the insurance is unsatisfactory or the premiums are unreasonably high, can order the freeholder to nominate another insurer.

'Period of Grace': When a dwelling is sold under the right to buy by a local authority or non-charitable housing association, the purchaser is given an estimate of service charges for the following five years. This estimate is the maximum recoverable during that time. Some purchasers under the right to buy have, however, had a very rude shock when the five year period of grace expires - see *Exceptionally High Service Charges* below.

d: The role of a recognised tenants' association
The tenants who are liable to pay for the provision of services may, if they wish, form a recognised tenants' association (RTA) under section 29 of the Landlord and Tenant Act 1985. Note that leaseholders count as tenants for this purpose (see Chapter One, where it explained that legally the two terms are interchangeable). If the freeholder refuses to give a notice recognising the RTA, it may apply for recognition to any member of the local Rent Assessment Committee panel ('Rent Assessment Committee' is the official term for a Leasehold Valuation Tribunal when it is carrying out certain functions, not otherwise relevant to leaseholders, under the Rent Act 1977).

An important benefit of having a RTA is that it has the right, at the beginning of the consultation process, to recommend persons or organisations that should be invited to submit estimates. However, the freeholder is under no obligation to accept these recommendations.

Another advantage is that the RTA can, whether the freeholder likes it or not, appoint a qualified surveyor to advise on matters relating to service charges. The surveyor has extensive rights to inspect the freeholder's documentation and take copies, and can enforce these rights in court if necessary.

Against these benefits must be set the principal disadvantage of having a RTA, namely that it weakens the freeholder's obligation to consult individual leaseholders. Where there is a RTA, the freeholder, instead of having to supply copies of the estimates to all leaseholders (or place copies where they are likely to be seen), merely has to send them to the secretary of the RTA, and the individual leaseholders must make do with summaries.

Leaseholders - and for that matter, ordinary periodic tenants - should therefore weigh carefully the advantages and disadvantages of setting up a RTA. If they decide against, there is nothing to prevent them from forming an *unrecognised* tenants' (or leaseholders') association, which can represent their interests to the freeholder, provided that it is made clear that formal recognition under section 29 is not being sought.

Challenging Service Charges

The Landlord and Tenant Act not only allows leaseholders to take action against unreasonable behaviour by the freeholder; it also enables them to take the initiative. This is done in two ways: by giving leaseholders rights to demand information, and by allowing them to challenge the reasonableness of the charge.

Any demand for service charges must include details about leaseholders' rights and how they can challenge the charges. If this is not done the leaseholder may withhold payment without penalty.

a: Right to information
Freeholders must provide a written summary of costs counting towards the service charge. It must be sent to the leaseholder within six months of the end of the period it covers. The service charge need not be paid until the summary is provided.

The law lays down some minimum requirements for the summary. It must:

- cover all the costs incurred during the twelve months it covers, even if they were included in service charge bills of an earlier or later period (see above for late charging and pre-charging);
- show how the costs incurred by the freeholder are reflected in the service charges paid, or to be paid, by leaseholders;
- say whether it includes any work covered by a grant (see above);
- distinguish: (a) those costs incurred for which the freeholder was not billed during the period; (b) those for which he was billed and did not pay; (c) those for which he paid bills.

If it covers five or more dwellings, the summary must, in addition, be certified by a qualified accountant as being a fair summary, complying with the Act, and supported by appropriate documentation.

The purpose of these rules is to put leaseholders in a position to challenge their service charges. After receiving the summary, the leaseholder has six months in which to ask the freeholder to make facilities available so that he can inspect the documents supporting the summary (bills, receipts, and so on) and take copies or extracts. The freeholder must make the facilities available within 21 days after such a request; the inspection itself must be free, although the freeholder can make a reasonable charge for the copies and extracts. Failure to provide these facilities, like failure to supply the summary, is punishable by a fine of up to £2500.

Very similar rules apply where the lease allows, or requires, the freeholder to take out insurance against certain contingencies, such as major repair, and to recover the premiums through the service charge. This is not unreasonable in itself and will, indeed, often be in the interests of leaseholders. The danger is, however, that the freeholder, knowing that the premiums are, in effect, being paid by someone else, has no incentive to shop around for the best deal. Section 30A of the Landlord and Tenant Act 1985 therefore lays down that leaseholders, or the secretary of the recognised tenants' association if there is one, may ask the freeholder for information about the policy. Failure to supply it, or to make facilities to inspect relevant documents available if requested to do so, is an offence incurring a fine of up to £2500.

It must be acknowledged that the rules allowing leaseholders to require information about service charges are, particularly in view of the £2500 fines, fairly onerous from the freeholder's point of view. It is the purpose of this book to inform leaseholders of their rights, not to make life difficult for freeholders: nevertheless, it must be admitted that if leaseholders wish to pursue a policy of confronting freeholders, and to cause them as much trouble as possible, sections 21, 22, and 30A offer plenty of scope.

b: Challenging a service charge
Any leaseholder liable to pay a service charge, and for that matter any freeholder levying one, may refer the charge to a Leasehold Valuation Tribunal to determine its reasonableness. This may be done at any time, even when the service in question is merely a proposal by the freeholder (for instance, for future major works). But the LVT will not consider a service charge if:

- it has already been approved by a court; or
- if the leaseholder has agreed to refer it to arbitration; or
- if the leaseholder has agreed it.

The first of these exceptions is obvious and the second is unlikely to apply very often. The third one is the problem: leaseholders should be careful, in their dealings with freeholders, to say or do nothing that could be taken to imply that they agree with any service charge that is in any way doubtful.

The LVT will consider:

- whether a service charge is payable and if so when, how, and by whom;
- whether the freeholder's costs of services, repairs, maintenance, insurance, or management are reasonably incurred;
- whether the services or works are of a reasonable standard; and

- whether any payment required in advance is reasonable.

The fees for application to a LVT can be obtained from the LVT and will usually change annually. Appeal against a LVT decision is not to the courts but to the Lands Tribunal.

By section 19 of the Landlord and Tenant Act 1985, any service charge deemed unreasonable by the LVT is irrecoverable by the freeholder. The determination of service charges by the LVT also plays an important part in the rules governing the use of forfeiture to recover service charges. It is to this that we now turn.

Forfeiture for Unpaid Service Charges

Forfeiture was mentioned at the end of Chapter Two. Briefly, it is the right of the freeholder to resume possession of the property if the leaseholder breaches the lease.

By section 81 of the Housing Act 1996, forfeiture for an unpaid service charge is available to the freeholder only if:

- the leaseholder has agreed the charge; or
- the charge has been upheld through post-dispute arbitration or by the Leasehold Valuation Tribunal or a court.

Regarding the first of these, it is necessary only to reiterate the warning to leaseholders to say or do nothing that could possibly be construed as representing their agreement to any service charge about whose legitimacy they have the slightest doubt.

Regarding the second, it should be noted that where the leaseholder has not agreed the service charge, proceedings before the LVT or a court or post-dispute arbitration are necessary before the freeholder can forfeit the lease.

A further requirement is that the amount of money involved must either exceed a certain amount or have been outstanding for a minimum period of time. The Government will set these limits by order. It is currently proposed that the minimum amount will be £350 and the minimum period three years, but this is yet to be confirmed. Note that it is necessary for only one of the requirements to be satisfied.

To sum up, before the leaseholder can forfeit:
- it must have been formally decided that the service charge is due,
- the amount must exceed the minimum amount or have been owed for the minimum time, and
- a section 146 notice must have been served (but this requirement does not apply if the service charge is reserved as rent).

The freeholder can still begin the process by issuing a section 146 notice (see Chapter Two) but it must state that the forfeiture cannot proceed until the requirements of section 81 have been met.

It remains to be seen how these new provisions will operate in practice. Their purpose is to prevent freeholders from using the draconian threat of forfeiture to pressurise leaseholders into paying disputed service charges, and to this extent the position of leaseholders has been greatly strengthened. The danger is that freeholders may respond by getting disputed charges before the LVT as quickly as possible so that forfeiture becomes available if the charges are upheld. Another concern is that some leaseholders, faced with service charges they are unwilling to pay but about which there is no dispute, may be unable to resist the temptation to invent spurious grounds for objection in order to deprive the freeholder of the weapon of forfeiture; this tactic is likely to provoke even relatively easy-going freeholders into legal action.

Once the leaseholder has agreed the service charge or it has been upheld by the LVT or a court or through arbitration, forfeiture becomes a serious threat and in this situation the advice can only be to pay the charge if at all possible. If, however, the leaseholder is unable to pay he may find it helpful to contact his mortgagee (if any). For the mortgagee, forfeiture is a disaster because it is likely to be left with a large unsecured debt on its hands, so many mortgagees in this situation will pay the service charges and add the cost to the outstanding mortgage. This does not solve the leaseholder's long term problem - that his lease commits him to payments he is unable to meet - but it will give him a little breathing space and may enable him to sell up and pay off his debts.

Some leaseholders, especially those of longer standing, may be living on fixed incomes and have very little cash to spare, even though their property is quite valuable. Sometimes their mortgage has been paid off altogether; even if it is still outstanding, it will probably be very small in relation to the value of the property. Leaseholders that find themselves in this 'property-rich, cash-poor' situation may find it helpful to look at equity release schemes, operated by a number of financial institutions.

Exceptionally High Service Charges
So far this Chapter has focused on service charges of normal proportions that, however unforeseen and unwelcome they may be, should be within the means of the great majority of leaseholders. A minority of leaseholders, however, face the much more serious problem of consistently very high service charges. Where the cause is sharp practice by the freeholder, or failure to observe the legal requirements, the leaseholder can look for protection to the Landlord and Tenant Act as described above. Often, however, the freeholder is not to blame: rather, the problem is that the work is genuinely necessary and unavoidably expensive. In this situation, and provided the landlord carefully follows the procedures laid down, the Landlord and Tenant Act offers no protection.

In what sort of housing is this most likely to occur? It is more likely to affect flats than houses because flats tend to contain potentially very expensive components such as lifts or communal arrangements for heating or ventilation. They are also more likely to have been built using construction methods or designs in vogue at one time but since found to lead to serious maintenance problems and high costs, whereas house building seems to be innately conservative and resistant to innovation: for instance, many blocks of flats contain asbestos, but very few houses.

All these problems apply to flats in general, but there is an additional problem with blocks of flats owned by local authorities and housing associations: namely that, unlike blocks of flats developed by commercial owners for sale, they are likely to combine rented properties, let to periodic tenants in the usual way, with leasehold properties, sold at some point in the past under the right to buy or some similar scheme. These 'mixed managed' blocks present special problems for both categories of resident as well as the freeholder.

The problems can be shown by taking a hypothetical example. **MUNICIPAL HEIGHTS** is a 15-storey tower block developed by the London Borough of Walford in the 1960s (when such things were fashionable). It contains 75 flats of which 60 are rented and 15 have been bought under the right to buy. In recent years its condition has deteriorated markedly: the lifts, having long exceeded their projected 25-year working life, have become hopelessly unreliable and urgently need to be replaced; the stairways, landings, and other communal areas need complete refurbishment; the windows need to be replaced; and asbestos has been found in the block. The tenants are understandably up in arms about their living conditions and are demanding action by the Council. The leaseholders, on the other hand, although also concerned about the state of the block, are well aware that the cost of necessary works has been reliably estimated at £3 000 000, working out to an average of £40 000 per dwelling, a sum none of them can possibly afford, and more than the value of the flats. The Council sympathises with their predicament but, on the other hand, some of the tenants are threatening it with legal action for failure to carry out its repairing obligations, and others are getting up a campaign to vote out the sitting Councillors in the forthcoming elections. So the Council, having carried out the consultation exercise required by the Landlord and Tenant Act, decides to go ahead and carry out the repairs. Now the Council's problem is that if it seeks to recover £40 000 each from the leaseholders, they will be unable to pay and the Council will have little option but to take legal action against them up to and including forfeiture; whereas if it makes no such attempt the debt will have to be met from elsewhere in the Housing Revenue Account, which, since Councils are no longer allowed to top up the HRA from general funds, means that it will be paid by the rents of Council tenants throughout the Borough, to which the Walford Federation of Tenants' Associations strongly objects.

One way out is for the government to come to the rescue. Sometimes, a council can obtain grants meeting some or all of the cost of improving run-down property. If this happened at Municipal Heights, the leaseholders' contributions could be considerably reduced, or even eliminated entirely. But funds of this kind are not available automatically; they have to be applied for, and come from a cash-limited budget. If the Council cannot get government funding, what then?

Clearly, there is no satisfactory way to resolve this problem. In a privately developed block, occupied wholly by leaseholders, the freeholder might possibly be prevailed upon to delay the repairs for a time if the leaseholders are prepared to put up with the poor conditions; but the Council can hardly be expected to take the same view when most of the residents are periodic tenants. Both the Council and the periodic tenants are likely to argue that the leaseholders are being asked to do no more than they agreed to do when they bought their leases. So the problems affecting Municipal Heights, and similar developments all over the country, are likely to rumble on for many years.

It is possible that the leaseholders will have redress if they can persuade a court that the local authority acted in bad faith at the time of the sale; if, for instance, Walford Council was well aware, but did not disclose, that there were, or might be, serious structural problems with Municipal Heights.

In most cases, however, Councils will be able to say, quite truthfully, that they had no idea of the problem when the sale took place, in which case the court is likely to apply the established legal principle of *caveat emptor* - 'let the buyer beware'.

All this book can do is warn prospective leaseholders of the serious problems that can arise in a minority of cases, and suggest some of the questions that they should ask before signing the lease.

1   **What is the condition of the building as a whole?** No one would buy a house, or an individual flat, without looking closely at its condition and estimating how much money it may need to have spent on it. But, when a flat is being bought, whether it is purpose-built or a conversion, it is equally important to look at the entire building of which it forms a part. The vendor should be asked for copies of past service charges, the freeholder should be asked whether major work is likely in the foreseeable future and what it is likely to cost, and an independent surveyor should be asked to report.

2   **What is the leaseholder's liability?** The lease will specify what the leaseholder must pay for. Sometimes it will require him to contribute to things from which he does not benefit. For example, it is common for even ground floor leaseholders to be expected to contribute to the costs of the lifts; and some leaseholders, having paid out of their own pockets to replace their windows, are outraged to discover, when the freeholder has the windows of the whole block renewed, that they are required to pay a share of the cost. Provisions such as these are much resented by many leaseholders, who argue that they are unfair; but the time to object to such unfairness is before signing the lease, not many years later when the bills come in. It is therefore essential that anyone proposing to enter into a lease should first consult a solicitor.

3   **Is there a 'period of grace' or other safeguard?** Right to buy leases contain an estimate of service charges for five years

following the sale and that is the maximum that the Council may charge. Many purchasers, reassured by this, have signed the lease without paying much attention to the likely level of service charges thereafter, expecting perhaps to have sold at a profit and moved on before the five years expire. If so, they have been reminded of what many people forgot during the 1980s: that property prices can go down as well as up. In short, it is unwise to rely on a 'period of grace' to provide anything other than short-term relief; and in particular it is unwise to speculate on the future behaviour of the housing market.

4 **What are the prospects for resale?** Traditionally, the homeowner's last resort in the face of overwhelming financial problems is to sell up in the expectation that the proceeds will suffice to pay off the mortgage, settle other outstanding debts such as service charges, and still leave something over. The stagnant property market of the early 1990s upset many calculations of this kind, but the much stronger market of recent years means that mortgages are often appreciably less than the value of the property, so for many people selling up offers a way out. So it is important to assess the salability of the dwelling by asking whether future purchasers are likely to be put off by anything about the flat itself or the block and district to which it belongs, and above all whether mortgage lenders are likely to look on it favourably.

15
ENFRANCHISEMENT AND EXTENSION OF LEASES

What Are Enfranchisement and Extension?
Chapter One set out the legal theory underlying the relationship between freeholder and leaseholder, and explained that a lease must be limited in time and that, in principle, at the end of that time the lease finishes and the property reverts to the freeholder.

It has always been, and still is, open to the freeholder and the leaseholder to negotiate some different arrangement. For instance, they might agree that the freeholder will buy the unexpired term of the lease from the leaseholder: but, because the freeholder and the leaseholder cannot be the same person, this will have the effect of extinguishing the lease and the leave the freeholder on sole possession of the land as if the lease had never existed. Alternatively, the freeholder might agree to sell the freehold to the leaseholder: again, and for the same reason, this will extinguish the lease, but this time it is the former leaseholder that will be left in sole freehold possession. The sale of the freehold to the leaseholder is called 'enfranchisement' of the lease, because it is freed, or 'enfranchised', from the overriding freehold, and replaces it. A further possibility is that the freeholder and leaseholder may agree to extend the lease beyond its original term. If agreements of this kind are negotiated, it is entirely for the freeholder and leaseholder to settle the conditions and the price.

In recent years, however, the law has forced freeholders, in certain circumstances, to sell freeholds or extend leases, whether they wish to or not. This has been done by three pieces of legislation: the Leasehold Reform Act 1967, the Landlord and Tenant Act 1987, and the Leasehold Reform, Housing and Urban Development Act 1993 (although all three Acts have been amended by later legislation, particularly the Housing Act 1996 and the Commonhold and Leasehold Reform Act 2002). The Acts are dealt with in the order they were passed, which means that the most important right - that of leaseholders of flats - is left to last. This is fitting, because, as is explained below, it was a Parliamentary afterthought; the Government originally had no intention of granting such an important right.

But before looking at the legislation, it is important to establish why extension and enfranchisement are important to the average leaseholder.

Extension of a Lease Some enlightened freeholders automatically extend the lease whenever it is assigned, so that if a lease that was originally granted for 125 years is assigned after 30, the assignee gets a lease not for 95 years, as one might expect, but for 125. From the leaseholder's point of view, such an arrangement is extremely valuable because otherwise the lease represents a wasting asset, whose value will drop sharply as the end of the term approaches. The arrangement can also benefit the freeholder by making the lease more valuable at the time of its original sale. But most leases are unaffected by assignment and would expire on the originally determined date were it not for legislation that obliges freeholders, in certain circumstances, to grant a fresh 90 year lease to the leaseholder: this is described below.

Individual Enfranchisement of a Lease Legislation, described below, now allows the leaseholder to acquire the freehold, in certain circumstances, whether or not the freeholder agrees. If not for this, the leaseholder would find that his home had reverted to the ownership of the freeholder at the end the lease and he would have to buy it back (assuming the freeholder were willing to sell). The freeholder is, however, entitled to compensation.

Collective Enfranchisement of Leases The problem with leasehold enfranchisement is that the property concerned must be capable of being held on a freehold basis. Where it stands on a distinct and definable piece of land this does not present a problem: the freehold of the land is transferred to the leaseholder and, as explained in Chapter One, any buildings on it are automatically transferred too. But if the property is only part of a larger building, it may not be attached to its own unique piece of land in the same way, so individual enfranchisement is not available to flat owners. If they wish to enfranchise, therefore, they have to agree among themselves that a single person or body will buy the freehold on behalf of all of them, while they continue to hold leases of their individual flats.

This is called 'collective enfranchisement', although this term is misleading because technically the leases have not been enfranchised at all: all that has happened is a change from the original freeholder to a new one nominated by the leaseholders. Since the passage of the Commonhold and Leasehold Reform Act 2002, this new freeholder has to be a special type of organisation called a 'Right to Enfranchise' (or 'RtE') company.

Rights to Enfranchise and Extend Leases: General Principles
The remainder of this Chapter sets out what rights leaseholders have if they wish to extend or enfranchise their leases. It is stressed at the outset, however, that anyone contemplating such a step should obtain independent legal advice from a solicitor, and in most cases also from a valuer. This applies not only if the lease is being enfranchised or extended under one of the Acts, but also if it is being done voluntarily by agreement with the freeholder. The issues involved are potentially very complex and attempting to deal with them without expert advice could put your home at risk. The Acts are available to what they describe as 'qualifying tenants': but the exact meaning of the term varies depending which right is being exercised under which Act. Usually, but not always, the term is defined in a way that excludes ordinary tenants and confines it to leaseholders. The key issue is the existence of a long lease (see below). Other former tests,

relating to residence or the amount of rent, were abolished by the 2002 Act.

A Long Lease For most purposes under the Acts, the leaseholder must own a lease originally granted for at least 21 years. Note that this is the term when the lease was granted, not the period it still has to run, so that a 99 year lease granted in 1910 is still a long lease in 2003 even though it has only six years to go. Recent legislation has put an end to a number of devices formerly inserted into leases by freeholders in order to avoid having to extend or enfranchise leases.

Some were bizarre: leases were made terminable on extraneous events, such as royal marriages or deaths, because the lease was not regarded as long if it depended on an event that could occur at any time. These evasions have been of no effect since the 1993 Act, which provides that leases containing them shall be treated as long leases.

Exemptions There are various exemptions from the Acts.
- If the freeholder is a charitable housing trust and the dwelling is provided as part of its charitable work, the leaseholder can neither extend nor enfranchise the lease (unless the charity agrees).
- The Acts do not apply to business leases. This applies even if a dwelling is included: for instance, if the lease of a shop includes the flat above it.
- The Acts do not apply if the property is within the precincts of a cathedral or owned by the Crown (however, it is possible that the Crown authorities will agree to a voluntary extension or enfranchisement of the lease). Some properties owned by the National Trust are also exempt.
- Other exemptions apply not across the board but to particular types of transaction. These are covered as the various Acts are discussed below.

Leasehold Reform Act 1967: Leases of Houses

The first legislation to deal with leasehold extension and enfranchisement was the Leasehold Reform Act 1967. This Act is still in force, but is not relevant to most residential leaseholders, who will get more benefit from later legislation. It can therefore be dealt with fairly briefly.

The Act relates only to residential leases of houses - not flats. With certain exceptions, a leaseholder qualifies to use it if he has held for at least two years a lease originally granted for 21 years or more. The Act allows qualifying leaseholders to acquire the freehold of their homes, or, if they prefer, extend the lease for 50 years.

The usual exemptions (see above) apply to the 1967 Act. In addition, it does not apply to most shared ownership leases granted by housing associations.

Most leaseholders qualifying to make use of the 1967 Act have long since done so, because the benefits of owning the freehold outweigh the drawback of having to pay the freeholder the difference (usually not very great) between the freehold and leasehold value of the house.

Generally speaking, therefore, remaining leasehold houses will be those to which the Act does not apply, either because the freeholder is exempt or because the house is attached to other property. The last point is an important limitation on the 1967 Act: if the land on which the house stands is shared by any other property not covered by the lease, however small it may be compared with the house, the Act cannot be used. It may, however, be possible for the leaseholder of such a house to use the new rights in the Leasehold Reform, Housing and Urban Development Act 1993.

The procedure for enfranchisement under the 1967 Act is as follows.

- The leaseholder serves a notice on the freeholder stating that he wishes to claim the freehold (or extend the lease). This notice should give particulars of the property and the lease.

- Within two months, the freeholder must send a counter notice that either accepts the leaseholder's claim or gives reasons for rejecting it. The freeholder may ask the leaseholder for a deposit of £25 or thrice the annual ground rent, whichever is more, and for proof that he holds the lease and meets the residence test. The leaseholder has 14 days to produce the money and 21 days to produce the proof.

- If the freeholder does not submit a counter notice within two months, the leaseholder's claim is automatically accepted. If the freeholder's counter notice unfairly rejects the leaseholder's claim, the leaseholder may apply to the county court.

Obviously, the freeholder is justified in rejecting the claim if the property does not come under the Act or if the leaseholder does not qualify. In addition, the freeholder may reject the claim if he acquired the house before 18th February 1966 and needs the house, on expiry of the lease, as a home for himself or a member of his family. He may also refuse to extend the lease (but not to enfranchise it) if he plans to redevelop the property.

Once it has been established that the leaseholder may enfranchise, a price must be agreed; if this is not possible, it will be set by a leasehold valuation tribunal. The Act lays down that the price should be the value of the freehold if it were being sold willingly but on the assumption that the lease were continuing and would be renewable under the Act. In effect, this formula means that the leaseholder is obliged to pay for what he is acquiring (the freehold) but not for what he has already got (the lease). Once a price has been agreed, or set by tribunal, either the freeholder or the leaseholder has one month to serve a notice on the other requiring him to complete. The freeholder must convey the freehold as a fee simple absolute, or (as a non-lawyer would say) outright.

Landlord and Tenant Act 1987: First Refusal and Mismanagement

The Landlord and Tenant Act 1987 was chiefly concerned with enabling leaseholders to protect themselves against unreasonable service charges, and it made numerous amendments to tighten the rules originally laid down in the Landlord and Tenant Act 1985 (see Chapter Three).

In addition, it granted leaseholders the important right of first refusal if the freehold of their property is sold. It also allowed leaseholders to acquire the freehold if the property is being mismanaged: however, this right is little used because of the difficult procedures involved, and although it remains on the statute book it is likely to fall into complete disuse because the 1993 Act has now given leaseholders the same right without having to prove mismanagement.

a: First refusal

The right of first refusal was granted in order to stop the practice of selling freeholds, without any reference to the leaseholders or other occupiers, from one person or organisation to another so that leaseholders were often completely in the dark about who the ultimate freeholder was (when this sort of thing went on the eventual freeholder often turned out to be a company existing on paper only and based somewhere completely inaccessible like the Cayman Islands - see Chapter Two for legislation passed at the same time forcing freeholders to give their name and an address in the UK for the service of legal notices). The right of first refusal remains important because it is sometimes available when ordinary collective enfranchisement, under the 1993 Act, is not possible.

The 1987 Act says that if the freeholder intends to sell the freehold he must first offer it to the leaseholders and other qualifying tenants. There are, however, some exceptions: the Act does not apply if the freeholder is selling to a member of his family, or if he lives in the block himself; nor does it apply if the block is not chiefly residential. In addition, virtually all public sector freeholders are excluded from the Act: this means local authorities, registered housing associations, and various other bodies. It is, however, unlikely that this sort of body will wish to sell its freehold. But if none of these exceptions applies, and if the majority of qualifying tenants (including leaseholders) wish to buy, they must be given the opportunity to meet the freeholder's price. For the purpose of defining a 'majority' there can be only one qualifying tenant in respect of each flat: in other words, joint tenants (or joint leaseholders) have only one 'vote' between them, and must agree between themselves how it will be used.

'Qualifying tenants' are:
- tenants entitled to a Fair Rent under the 1977 Rent Act: that is, most tenants of self-contained dwellings holding a tenancy originally granted on or before 14th January 1989, but excluding council tenants; and
- leaseholders, except for business leaseholders (the normal 21 year minimum does not apply).

If the qualifying tenants and freeholder cannot agree terms for the sale, the freeholder is able to sell to someone else. However, the qualifying tenants must be informed of this sale and, most importantly, of the price. They then have the right to buy the freehold from the new owner at whatever price he paid. This is designed to stop the original freeholder from asking the qualifying tenants for an excessive price that they are bound to reject, then selling to someone else at a lower price. Similarly, if the freeholder carries out a sale without informing the qualifying tenants, they have the right to buy from the new freeholder for the same price that he paid. Procedure under the 1987 for the right of first refusal is as follows.

* The freeholder notifies all qualifying tenants of his desire to sell and of the price at which he is willing to do so (including any non-monetary element). The notice must state the proposed method of sale: for instance, by conveyance or by auction.

*   The freeholder must give the qualifying tenants at least two months to respond; and, if they say they wish to buy, at least a further two months (28 days if the sale is to be by auction) to come up with a nominee purchaser to acquire the freehold on their behalf. This could conceivably be in an individual or an organisation that already exists, but is much likelier to be a company set up specially for the purpose by the qualifying tenants, and under their control.

*   During this period, the landlord and the qualifying tenants may wish to take the opportunity to negotiate the price.

*   If a majority of the qualifying tenants have put forward a nominee purchaser and agreed with the freeholder on a price, the freeholder may not sell to anyone else.

*   If the qualifying tenants fail to put forward a nominee purchaser, or if a mutually acceptable price is not agreed, the freeholder has twelve months to sell to someone else in accordance with the original notice (by auction, if that was the method specified; and in any other case for a price not less than that originally offered to the qualifying tenants). If no sale has taken place within twelve months, the freeholder must start the procedure again from scratch if he wishes to sell.

b: Mismanagement: the right to enfranchise
As mentioned above, the 1987 Act is designed mainly to protect leaseholders against mismanagement and sharp practice by freeholders. It therefore gives them the power of collective enfranchisement against a freeholder guilty of serious or repeated breach of his obligations. The power is available to long leaseholders, but a leaseholder does not qualify to use this part of the Act if he owns long leases of three or more flats in the block.

Moreover, this part of the 1987 Act does not apply where the freeholder is the Crown or a public body such as a local authority or a registered housing association. Nor does it apply when the freeholder resides in the property himself. It is available only where two-thirds or more of the flats in the block are let on long leases, and in blocks of ten flats or fewer a higher proportion is required. The court can make an order transferring the freehold to the leaseholders' nominee only if a manager appointed (see Chapter Two) by a court or LVT has controlled the premises for at least two years, unless the leaseholders can show both

- that the freeholder is and is likely to remain in breach of his obligations under the lease; and
- that the mere appointment of a manager would be an inadequate remedy.

All these restrictions suggest that the Act envisages that enfranchisement on grounds of mismanagement is very much a last resort; indeed, it is necessary for the leaseholders to take their case to court and get permission before they can proceed. The right was seldom used and, although it remains available in theory, in practice it has been superseded by the 1993 Act, which gives most leaseholders the right of collective enfranchisement whatever the standard of management and with no need for a court order. Nevertheless, it is just possible there is a body of leaseholders somewhere willing to use the 1987 Act rather than the 1993 Act. The procedures for collective enfranchisement following mismanagement are therefore briefly set out here, with a warning that the general recommendation to employ a solicitor applies with special emphasis if this route is chosen.

- At least two-thirds of the qualifying leaseholders must serve a preliminary notice informing the freeholder that they intend to go to court to acquire the freehold. The notice must give the names and addresses of the leaseholder and the grounds for their application; the freeholder should also be given a reasonable deadline to rectify the problems if it is possible for him to do so.

- The leaseholders must apply to the court, giving their reasons for dissatisfaction and requesting an order to transfer the freehold to their nominee purchaser (probably, as with other forms of collective enfranchisement, a company set up for the purpose).

- If satisfied that it is fair to do so, the court will transfer the block to the nominee purchaser. The price will have to be agreed by the leaseholders and the freeholder; or, if (as is likely) this is not possible, by a Leasehold Valuation Tribunal. The price will be the value of the freehold on the assumption that all the leases are to continue: there will be no additional 'marriage value' (see below), and this is one of the few reasons for preferring to use the 1987 Act rather than the 1993 Act.

Leasehold Reform, Housing and Urban Development Act 1993: Collective Enfranchisement and Lease Extension

The 1993 Act greatly extended the rights of leaseholders: its passage through Parliament was, indeed, strongly contested by large private freeholders, who claimed that it was unfair to them as property owners. It made a number of adjustments, dealt with above, to existing rights under the 1967 and 1987 Acts; in addition, it created two new rights for leaseholders of flats. These are the right to collective enfranchisement, and the right to extend individual leases.

a: Collective enfranchisement under the 1993 Act

In outline, the right to collective enfranchisement under the 1993 Act is similar to, but much easier than, collective enfranchisement under the 1987 Act. Under both schemes, qualifying leaseholders choose a purchaser to whom the freeholder can be forced to sell; but under the 1993 Act there is no need for a court order and no need to show that there has been mismanagement.

The 1993 Act is available to long leaseholders, provided that at least two-thirds of the flats are let on long leases and at least half the eligible leaseholders are involved.

However, the block may not be enfranchised if it falls within the normal exemptions, or if it is not chiefly residential, or if it is a house converted into four flats or fewer with a resident freeholder who owned the freehold before the conversion. Even if there is a resident freeholder, however, the scheme applies to houses converted into five flats or more and to purpose-built blocks even if they contain only two flats.

There are special provisions for any parts of the building that are occupied by people or organisations other than qualifying leaseholders. Some flats may be let to periodic tenants, for instance, and a block that faces a main road may well contain shop units on the ground floor. Any such parts may, and in some cases must, be leased back to the original freeholder when the block is acquired. 'Leaseback', as it is called, is mandatory for any flats let to periodic tenants (secure or assured) by a local authority or a registered housing association. This means that they can continue as council (or association) tenants, and do not lose any legal rights. It is up to the freeholder (not the leaseholders) whether he wants a leaseback of other flats or premises, such as business units or flats occupied by non-qualifying leaseholders. Unless the parties agree otherwise, leaseback is for 999 years at a notional rent - in other words, on terms typical of residential leases, and discussed in Chapters One and Two.

The leaseholders must choose a purchaser. Formerly, this could be any individual or organisation that had the confidence of the others and was willing to undertake the role. The 2002 Act has, however, tightened the rules by providing that only a 'Right to Enfranchise' ('RtE') company can take over the freehold. This protects leaseholders' rights by ensuring that the enfranchisee is a body in which they all have a right to be involved, but the Government has taken powers to lay down what the constitution of the RtE company must be, and it is likely that many leaseholders will find the prescribed constitution unwieldy and inflexible.

Setting up and running the RtE company is only one of the responsibilities in which collective enfranchisement will involve leaseholders. They will also have to pay both their own and the freeholder's legal and professional costs. And above all, they must pay the purchase price of the freehold, which, unless they come to an agreement with the freeholder, will be decided by a leasehold valuation tribunal in accordance with rules laid down in the Act. These say that the price consists of two components: the open market value and the 'marriage value'.

According to the formula in the Act, the **open market value** should reflect the income the freeholder would have received from rents plus the prospect of regaining possession of the parts of the building currently let. How much this is will depend on how the building is being used now. If, as will often be the case, it consists wholly of flats let on long leases with many years to run, the open market value will probably be low because ground rents are usually very modest and the prospect of regaining possession is a distant one and of correspondingly little value. But if the building contains lucrative business or periodic tenancies, perhaps quite short term, and if the freeholder elects not to have these leased back, the open market value will be substantial.

The other component in the price, the **'marriage value'**, is based on the assumption that, combined (as they will be after enfranchisement), the leases and the freehold have a greater value than they would if sold separately. The Act says the freeholder is entitled to half this amount. In most cases, however, especially where the leases have a long time to run, the marriage value will be low, and where a lease has more than 80 years to run the marriage value will be disregarded. Altogether the costs of enfranchisement may be considerable. It is therefore prudent for leaseholders to explore the ground before committing themselves. This can be done by any qualifying leaseholder by serving a notice on the freeholder (or whomever the leaseholder pays rent to) under section 11 of the Act. Such a notice obliges the freeholder to disclose, within 28 days, information that will be relevant to any sale, such as title deeds, surveyor's reports, planning restrictions, and so on. This will allow the leaseholders to take an informed view of whether they wish to go for collective enfranchisement and, if so, on what terms. At this stage, they should take their time and think it over carefully, for if they proceed further they will be obliged to pay the freeholder's legal costs if they later decide to withdraw.

It may be appropriate, too, at this stage, for the leaseholders to ask the freeholder whether he is prepared to consider a voluntary sale without forcing all concerned to go through the somewhat elaborate procedures laid down by the 1993 Act. A reasonable freeholder, since he will be aware that he can be forced to sell anyway, may well be willing to discuss this.

If the leaseholders decide to go ahead with collective enfranchisement under the 1993 Act, they must form a 'Right to Enfranchise' ('RtE') company. The purpose of the company is to act as the vehicle for the enfranchisement and subsequently to own the freehold of the block.

Every RtE company has to operate in accordance with a constitution (the 'memorandum and articles') laid down by Government. The aim is to ensure that all leaseholders have a fair chance to take part, but it is likely that many leaseholders will find that the constitution laid down for them is extremely bureaucratic and unwieldy, especially when it is remembered that many enfranchisements will be carried out in small blocks where they may be only a dozen leaseholders or even fewer.

All qualifying leaseholders are entitled to be members of the RtE company, but in practice it is controlled by 'participating members', namely those leaseholders that have served on the company a 'participation notice'. When the company is set up all qualifying leaseholders must be sent a formal notice inviting them to participate by serving such a notice. Once the enfranchisement takes place, membership of the RtE company is confined to participating members.

The RtE company serves an initial notice (also called a 'section 13 notice') giving the names and addresses of the leaseholders involved and exactly specifying what property they wish to enfranchise and

Enfranchisement and Extension of Leases

which parts, if any, they will lease back. The notice must also propose a price, and give the freeholder at least two months to reply. Once the initial notice has been served, the freeholder may not sell the freehold to any third party.

From now on, the RtE company handles proceedings on behalf of the leaseholders. The freeholder may require the RtE company to provide evidence to show that the participating leaseholders are qualified under the Act. If the RtE company does not respond within 21 days, the freeholder may in some circumstances treat the initial notice as being withdrawn.

By the date specified in the initial notice, the freeholder must serve a counter notice either accepting the leaseholders' right to enfranchise or giving reasons for rejecting it. The freeholder must also state whether he accepts the details of the leaseholders' proposal as regards price and exactly what is to be included in the sale, and must say whether he wishes to lease back any parts of the property (in addition to those where leaseback is mandatory). The freeholder may refuse to exercise his right to lease back parts of the premises let on lucrative business lets because the effect of this will be to increase the price and, perhaps, deter the leaseholders from continuing. In the unlikely event that most of the leaseholders' leases have less than five years to run, the freeholder has the right to stop the enfranchisement if he can satisfy a court that he intends to redevelop the block.

The intention of the Act is that after the freeholder's counter notice the parties will attempt to resolve any differences, so that the sale of the freehold can proceed on agreed terms. Often, however, agreement will be impossible and in that case the matters in dispute are referred to a leasehold valuation tribunal. Such a referral must take place at least two months, and not more than six months, after the freeholder's counter notice; if no agreement is reached, and no referral made, after six months, the initial notice will be deemed withdrawn.

Once the terms have been settled, the parties have two months to exchange contracts. At the end of this time, the nominee purchaser has a further two months to ask a court to transfer the freehold on the terms agreed (or determined by the tribunal); or the freeholder may ask the court to rule that the initial notice shall be treated as being withdrawn.

To sum up, the procedure is complex and demanding, which is why it has been little used even though several years have passed since it became available under the 1993 Act. The 2002 Act has made the process more favourable to leaseholders in some ways, but these improvements are more than offset by the further layer of difficulty added by the new requirement to set up a RtE company. All in all, it seems likely that these procedures will not be much used, but their existence may be helpful in persuading freeholders to negotiate seriously if leaseholders want to buy the freehold.

b: Lease extension under the 1993 Act
Although the right to collective enfranchisement, as created by the 1993 Act, is of great importance because it makes a fundamental shift in the relationship between freeholders and leaseholders, the complex procedures mean that it is likely to be relatively seldom used. On the other hand, the right to a new lease, which was also created (for flat owners) by the 1993 Act, is likely to prove of immense practical benefit to thousands of leaseholders, not least because it can be exercised on an individual basis. It is ironic that this, the most valuable right leaseholders derive from the 1993 Act, was something of a Parliamentary afterthought. The original intention was to create the right to collective enfranchisement, with individual lease extensions as very much a second best option available only to leaseholders that for some reason were disqualified from collective enfranchisement. But as the legislation made its way through Parliament the right to extend leases was granted to more and more categories of leaseholder, and by the time the Act became law it had become a general right.

The principle is similar to the right to lease extension that house owners enjoy under the 1967 Act. Anyone that has owned for at least two years a long lease of a flat qualifies to extend it under the 1993 Act. The former low rent test and residence test were abolished by the 2002

Act. The freeholder is required to grant a new lease running for the remainder of the term of the old lease plus an additional 90 years, so that if the old lease had 40 years to go the new one will be granted for 130. In other respects, however, the terms of the new lease will be the same as, or very similar to, the old one.

The leaseholder will have to pay the freeholder a sum consisting of two components calculated in accordance with rules set out in the Act. The first represents the reduction in the market value of the freehold that results because the freeholder will now have to wait to regain possession for 90 years longer than would otherwise have been the case. The less time the old lease had to run, the higher this component is likely to be. The second component is the 'marriage value', reflecting the higher value of a longer lease. As with collective enfranchisement, the freeholder is entitled to 50% of the marriage value, but it is disregarded altogether if the old lease has more than 80 years to go.

A leaseholder who is contemplating a lease extension should begin by serving a preliminary notice on the freeholder. This has the same function as with collective enfranchisement: it commits the leaseholder to nothing, but requires the freeholder to supply within 28 days the information that will enable the leaseholder to decide whether to go ahead.

The procedure is modelled on that for collective enfranchisement:

- The leaseholder serves an initial notice (a 'section 42 notice') on the freeholder. This must give details of the property concerned as well as of the leaseholder and his claim to qualify to use the 1993 Act. It must state how much the leaseholder proposes to pay, and set a date, at least two months ahead, by which the freeholder must reply. Once the notice has been served, the leaseholder must allow the freeholder to have access to the flat for the purpose of valuation.

- The freeholder must either agree that the leaseholder qualifies under the Act, or give reasons for disagreeing. If the freeholder agrees that the leaseholder is qualified to extend the lease, he may still suggest a that price of the new lease, or its other terms, should be different to the leaseholder's proposals. The freeholder can go to court for permission to reject the extension entirely if the current lease has less than five years to run and the freeholder then intends to redevelop the property.

- The freeholder and leaseholder should then attempt to resolve any differences by negotiation. If agreement is not reached, the question may be referred to the leasehold valuation tribunal at lease two months, and not less than six months, after the freeholder's counter notice. If, six months after the counter notice, there is neither an agreement nor a referral to a tribunal, the leaseholder's initial notice will be deemed withdrawn. In this event the leaseholder is liable for any reasonable expenses incurred by the freeholder.
- Once the terms are settled, either by negotiation or by the tribunal, the parties have two months to exchange contracts. If exchange does not take place during this period, the leaseholder has a further two months to apply to court for an order extending the lease on the terms agreed (or laid down by a tribunal).

It should be noted that collective enfranchisement takes priority over individual lease extensions, so that the effect of an initial notice of collective enfranchisement is to freeze, for the time being, any current claims to extend leases. If the collective enfranchisement fails to go ahead, the extension claims resume where they left off.

16

RELATIONSHIP BREAKDOWN AND HOUSING RIGHTS

When a relationship breaks down, whether the people in question are married or not, problems can often occur in relation to the property that was home. The rights of people will depend mainly on whether they are married or not, whether there are children involved and the legal status of individuals in the home.

Housing rights in an emergency

In the main, it is women who suffer from domestic violence. This section refers to women but the rights are the same for men.

If you are women and have been threatened by a man and are forced to leave your home then there are several possibilities for action in an emergency. The first of these is either going to a women's refuge. These provide shelter, advice and emotional support for women and children. These refuges will always try to admit you and as a result are sometimes crowded. They will always try to find you somewhere to live in the longer term. Refuges have a 24-hour telephone service if you need to find somewhere. For addresses see *useful addresses* at the back of this book.

Approaching the council

A person suffering domestic violence who has been forced to flee can approach the local council and ask for help as a homeless person. Councils will demand proof of violence and you will need to get evidence from a professional person, such as doctor or social worker or police. The council decides whether or not it has a duty to help you and you should seek advice if they refuse. Some councils, but not all will offer help to battered women. If you are accepted as homeless then the council should not send you back to the area where the violence began.

Obtaining a court order

Another course of action in an emergency is to obtain a court order against the man you live with. Courts can issue orders stating that a man:

- Should not assault you or harass you
- Not to assault any children living with you
- To leave the home and not to return
- To keep a certain distance from your home or any other place where your children go regularly.
- To let you back in your home if you have been excluded.

If you believe a court order would help you should get advice on where to find a solicitor or law centre that deals with these types of applications to the court. Certain orders are harder to get than others, such as exclusion orders. Matters need to be very serious indeed before such an order will be made. However, you will be advised of this when approaching a solicitor or law centre.

Failure to obey the terms and conditions laid down in the order can lead to arrest for contempt and a fine or even imprisonment.

Long term rights to the home

Long term rights to stay in a home depend on a number of circumstances. If you are married and the ownership or tenancy of the property is in joint names you have equal rights to live in the property. If it is owned then you will have a right to a share of the proceeds if it is sold. In certain circumstances have a right to more (or less) than a half share, or to the tenancy in your name after divorce.

If you are married but the ownership or tenancy is in one name only there are laws to protect the rights of the other party. Courts have the power to decide who has the ownership or rights over the matrimonial home, even if the property is held in one persons name only. This can also apply to people who were married but are now divorced and to those who were planning to get married within three years of their engagement.

Spouses who are not the owner or tenant of the home have a right to stay there. The court has the power to exclude either of the spouses, even if they are sole or joint owner or tenant. If your husband has left and stopped paying the rent or mortgage payments, the landlord or building society is obliged to accept payments from you, if you wish to make them, even if the property is not in your name. If the home is owned by your husband then you can register your right to live in it. This prevents your husband selling the home before the court has decided who should live there. And also prevents him taking out a second mortgage on the property without your knowledge. This is known as 'registering a charge' on the home. The court also has the power to transfer a fully protected private tenancy, an assured tenancy or a council or housing association tenancy from one partner to another.

If the matrimonial home is owner occupied and proceedings have started for a divorce, the court will decide how the value of the property will be divided up. The law recognises that, even if the property is in the husbands name only, the wife has a right to a share in its value, that she often makes a large unpaid contribution through housework or looking after children and that this should be recognised in divorce proceedings. The court looks at a number of things when reaching a decision:

- The income and resources of both partners
- The needs of you and your husband
- The standard of living that you and your husband had before the marital breakdown
- Ages of partners and length of marriage
- Contributions to the welfare of the family

- Conduct of partners
- Loss of benefits that you might have had if the marriage had not have broken down.

The court also has to consider whether there is any way that they can make a 'clean break' between you and you husband so that there are no further financial ties between you.

In certain circumstances, the court can order sale of the matrimonial home and the distribution of proceed between partners.

If you are not married

If you are not married then your rights will depend on who is the tenant or the owner of the home.

Tenants

If a tenancy is in joint names then you both have equal rights to the home. You can exclude your partner temporarily as we have seen by a court order. If you are a council tenant then you may want to see if you can get the council to rehouse you. You should get advice on this from an independent agency (see useful addresses).

If the tenancy is in your partners name only then the other person can apply for the right to stay there, for their partner to be excluded or for the tenancy to be transferred.

Home owners

If you live in an owner occupied property you and you partner may have certain rights to a share of the property even if you are not married.

If the home is jointly owned then you have a clear right to a share in its value. If one person has contributed moiré than the other then a court can decide that an equal share is unfair. The court cannot order the transfer of the ownership of property but it can order the sale and distribution of the proceeds.

If the home is in one persons name there is no automatic right to live in the home, even if there are children. However, a solicitor acting on your behalf can argue that by virtue of marriage and contribution you should be allowed to stay there and be entitled to a share.

17

HOUSING ADVICE

General advice
Citizens Advice Bureaus, which are situated throughout the U.K., provide advice on all problems, including housing and other matters such as legal, welfare benefits and relationship breakdown. If appropriate they can refer you for more specialist help to a solicitor or advice agency. This advice is free of charge. To find a local office, look in the telephone directory under National Association of Citizens Advice Bureau.

Housing Advice Centres
In many areas there are specialist advice centres offering housing aid and advice. The service they offer varies from one-off information to detailed help over a long period. There are two main types of housing advice centres, Local council housing aid centres which can advise on all kinds of problems, although they will not be able to take action against their own council. Independent housing aid centres may be better equipped to do this. These centres can offer detailed assistance over a length of time and also one-off advice. There are a number of independent housing aid centres throughout the country operated by Shelter. You should contact Shelter for you're nearest centre.

Other specialist advice
Law centres-they offer free advice and can sometimes represent you in court. They can usually advise on all aspects of law and also advise battered women. They cannot, however, take divorce cases. For this you will need a solicitor. Shelter can provide a list of law centres.

For advice on welfare rights you should try the local council, who may employ a welfare rights advisor. Advisers can also contact the advice line which is run by the Child Poverty Action Group. For women's rights the Women's Aid Federation England and Welsh Women's Aid refer battered women, with or without children, to refuges. They can put you in touch with sympathetic solicitors and local women's aid groups and can offer a range of other advice, such as welfare benefits.

For immigration advice, the Joint Council for the Welfare of Immigrants offers advice on all types of problems connected with immigration and nationality. The United Kingdom Immigrants Advisory Service offers advice and help on problems with immigration. The Refugee Council has an advice service for refugees and asylum seekers.

Advice from solicitors

Solicitors can advise you on all aspects of the law, represent you in certain courts and, if necessary, get a barrister to represent you. It is best to find a solicitor who specialises in housing rights as they usually have a wider knowledge of specific areas. You can get a list of solicitors who specialise in housing law from the Community Legal Service (CLS) Directory in your local library. The list is also on the CLS website. Citizens Advice Bureaus can also supply specialist solicitor details.

Free advice and help

The legal Help Scheme can pay for up to two hours worth of free advice and assistance and for matrimonial cases up to three hours. The scheme is means tested and you must come withy the limits of the scheme to qualify. For details of the scheme you should approach a Citizens Advice Bureau or a solicitors practice operating the scheme. You must have reasonable grounds for defending an action. In certain cases, if you succeed in obtaining cash compensation then you may have to pay a proportion of it back, this is known as the *statutory charge*.

GLOSSARY

A SUMMARY OF IMPORTANT TERMS

FREEHOLDER: Someone who owns their property outright.

LEASEHOLDER: Someone who has been granted permission to live on someone else's land for a fixed term.

TENANCY: One form of lease, the most common types of which are fixed-term or periodic.

LANDLORD: A person who owns the property in which the tenant lives.

LICENCE: A licence is an agreement entered into whereby the landlord is merely giving you permission to occupy his/her property for a limited period of time.

TRESPASSER: Someone who has no right through an agreement to live in a property.

PROTECTED TENANT: In the main, subject to certain exclusions, someone whose tenancy began before 15th January 1989.

ASSURED TENANT: In the main, subject to certain exclusions, someone whose tenancy began after 15th January 1989.

NOTICE TO QUIT: A legal document giving the protected tenant twenty eight days notice that the landlord intends to apply for possession of the property to the County Court.

GROUND FOR POSSESSION: One of the stated reasons for which the landlord can apply for possession of the property.

MANDATORY GROUND: Where the judge must give possession of the property.

DISCRETIONARY GROUND: Where the judge may or may not give possession, depending on his own opinion.

STUDENT LETTING: A tenancy granted by a specified educational institution.

HOLIDAY LETTING: A dwelling used for holiday purposes only.

ASSURED SHORTHOLD TENANCY: A fixed-term post-1989 tenancy.

PAYMENT OF RENT: Where you pay a regular sum of money in return for permission to occupy a property or land for a specified period of time.

FAIR RENT: A rent set by the Rent Officer every two years for most pre-1989 tenancies and which is lower than a market rent.

MARKET RENT: A rent deemed to be comparable with other non-fair rents in the area.

RENT ASSESSMENT COMMITTEE: A committee set up to review rents set by either the Rent Officer or the landlord.

PREMIUM: A sum of money charged for permission to live in a property.

DEPOSIT: A sum of money held against the possibility of damage to property.

QUIET ENJOYMENT: The right to live peacefully in your own Home.

REPAIRS: Work required to keep a property in good order.

IMPROVEMENTS: Alterations to a property.

LEGAL AID: Help with your legal costs, which is dependent on income.

HOUSING BENEFIT: Financial help with rent, which is dependent on income.

HOUSING ADVICE CENTRE: A center which exists to give advice on housing-related matters and which is usually local authority-funded.

LAW CENTRE: A center, which exists for the purpose of assisting the public with legal advice.

Appendix 1 – Useful addresses
Age Concern England
Astral House
1268 London Road SW16 4ER
020 8679 8000

Building Societies Association
3 Seville Row
London W15 3PB
020 7437 065

Child Poverty Action Group
94 White Lion Street
London N1 9PF
020 7235 6569

Commission for Racial Equality
Elliot House
1-12 Arlington Street
London SW1E 5EH
020 7828 7022

Consumers Association
2 Marylebone Road
London NW1 4DF
020 7830 6000

Disability Alliance
Universal House
88-94 Wentworth Street
London E1 7SA
020 7247 8776

Equal Opportunities Commission
Arndale House
Arndale Centre
Manchester
M4 3EQ
0845 601 5901

Federation of Black Housing Organisations
Second Floor
1 King Edwards Road
London E9 7SF
020 8533 7053

Gay and Lesbian Switchboard
020 7837 7342

Homeless Link
Alliance House
12 Caxton Street
London SW1H OQS
020 7357 6917

The Housing Corporation
149 Tottenham Court Road
London W1P OBN
020 7357 6917

Immigration Advisory Service
County House
190 Great Dean Street
London SE1 4YB
020 7357 6917

The Independent Housing Ombudsman
Norman House
105-109 The Strand
London WC2R OAA
020 7836 3630

Leasehold Advisory Service
70-74 City Road
London EC1V 9JR
020 7833 2931

Legal Action Group
242 Pentonville Road
London N1 9UN
020 7403 3888

National Council for Civil Liberties
21 Tabard Street
London SE1 4LA
020 7403 3888

Prisoners Wives and Families Association
254 Caledonian Road
London N1 ONG
020 7278 3981

Women's Aid Federation Helpline
PO Box 391
Bristol BS9 7WS
0117 944 4411

Assignment of leases 88
Assured tenants 23
Assured shorthold tenancy 20 25

Bedsits 14
Breaching a lease 89

Challenging service charges 101
Collective enfranchisements of leases 112
Company lets 10
Common part grants 50
Commonhold 72
Commonhold and Leasehold Reform Act 2002 65
Consultation with leaseholders 95
Contracts 17
Council tax 36

Date of commencement of tenancy 1 7
Damages 43
Deposits 38
Different types of tenancy agreement 20
Disabled tenants 48
DSS 12
Dwellings exempt from council tax 37

Ending a tenancy 18 52
Enfranchisement and extension of leases 111
Eviction 41
Exceptionally high service charges 106

Fast Track possession 30
Forfeiture for unpaid service charges 104
Freehold 15 65
Furniture

Going to court 55
Grounds for possession of a tenancy 27

Head leases 71
Holiday lets 13
Housing advice 135
1-lousing association tenancies 59
Housing benefit 34
Houses in multiple occupation 48
Housing rights in an emergency 129

individual enfranchisement of a lease 112
Injunctions 43
Insurance 52 99
Introductory tenancies 59

Joint tenancies 31
Landlord and Tenant Act 1987 117
Landlord obligations 18
Leasehold Reform Act 115
Leasehold Reform, Housing and Urban Development Act 1993 121
Leasehold 16 65
Leasehold valuation tribunals 90
Letting agents 9

Mismanagement: the right to enfranchise 119
Mixed tenure blocks 69

Obligations of freeholder and leaseholder 73
Overcrowding 20

Payment of rent 30 33
Powers of leaseholders over management 84
Protected tenancy 20

Public sector tenancies 57

Recognised tenants associations 88
Relationship breakdown and housing rights 129
Renovation grants 49
Rent books 19
Rent control for assured tenants 33
Repairs and improvements 45
Reporting repairs to a landlord 46
Restrictions on housing benefit 35
Right to buy 57
Right to manage 85
Right to quiet enjoyment of a home 41
Right to repair and make improvements 58
Right to succeed 58

Sanitation health and hygiene 49
Secure tenancies 57
Security of tenure 27
Services provided under the tenancy 18 52
Service charges 37 91
Shared Ownership 70
Short lets 11
Squatters 21
Student lets 12
Sub leases 71

Tenancy agreement 18
Tenancies that are not assured 24
Tenancies in Scotland 61

Tenants obligations 18
Tenants rights whilst improvements are being carried out 47
Tenants rights to make improvements 47

The law and owner occupiers 65
Types of leasehold property 68

Unreasonable service charges 94

Viewing a Property 14

www.straightforwardco.co.uk

All titles, listed below, in the Straightforward Guides Series can be purchased online, using credit card or other forms of payment by going to www.straightfowardco.co.uk A discount of 25% per title is offered with online purchases.

Law
A Straightforward Guide to:
Consumer Rights
Bankruptcy Insolvency and the Law
Employment Law
Private Tenants Rights
Family law
Small Claims in the County Court
Contract law
Intellectual Property and the law
Divorce and the law
Leaseholders Rights
The Process of Conveyancing
Knowing Your Rights and Using the Courts
Producing Your own Will
Housing Rights
The Bailiff the law and You
Probate and The Law
Company law
What to Expect When You Go to Court
Guide to Competition Law
Give me Your Money-Guide to Effective Debt Collection
Caring for a Disabled Child

General titles
Letting Property for Profit

Buying, Selling and Renting property
Buying a Home in England and France
Bookkeeping and Accounts for Small Business

Creative Writing
Freelance Writing
Writing Your own Life Story
Writing performance Poetry
Writing Romantic Fiction
Speech Writing

Teaching Your Child to Read and write
Teaching Your Child to Swim
Raising a Child-The Early Years

Creating a Successful Commercial Website
The Straightforward Business Plan
The Straightforward C.V.
Successful Public Speaking

Handling Bereavement
Play the Game-A Compendium of Rules
Individual and Personal Finance
Understanding Mental Illness
The Two Minute Message
Guide to Self Defence
Buying a Used Car
Tiling for Beginners

Go to:
www.straightforwardco.co.uk